D0849449

DEC 2006
LI

Careers in Focus

Cosmetology

Ferguson
An imprint of ✓ Facts On File

Ferguson
An imprint of Facts On File, Inc.
132 West 31st Street
New York NY 10001

Library of Congress Cataloging-in-Publication Data

Careers in focus. Cosmetology.—3rd ed.
    p. cm.
Includes index.
ISBN 0-89434-472-2 (hardcover : alk. paper)
1. Beauty culture—Vocational guidance—United States. 1. Ferguson
Publishing Company. II. Title: Cosmetology.
TT958 .C367 2003
646.7'2'02373—dc21   2002012339

Ferguson books are available at special discounts when purchased in bulk quantities for businesses, associations, institutions, or sales promotions. Please call our Specia Sales Department in New York at (212) 967-8800 or (800) 322-8755.____

You can find Ferguson Publishing on the World Wide Web at
http://www.fergpubco.com

Cover photo courtesy Daniel Bosler/Tony Stone Images

Printed in the United States of America

MP 10 9 8 7 6 5 4 3

This book is printed on acid-free paper.

Table of Contents

Introduction 1

Aromatherapists 5

Barbers 17

Color Analysts and Image Consultants 25

Cosmetic Surgeons 33

Cosmeticians 46

Cosmetics Sales Representatives 56

Cosmetologists 62

Dermatologists 74

Electrologists 84

Makeup Artists 93

Massage Therapists 103

Mortuary Cosmetologists 114

Nail Technicians 125

Salon Managers 136

Spa Attendants 145

State Boards of Cosmetology 155

Index 171

Introduction

From a new summer 'do to a milk and honey facial, from a leg waxing to an eyebrow plucking, cosmetologists provide a wide range of beauty and health services. Back when a shave and a haircut cost two bits, men spent their lunch hours relaxing in hydraulic barber chairs for hot, aromatic shaves. Meanwhile, women got their hair done in beauty salons, while also indulging in occasional manicures and facials. This attention to skin care and hair care is no longer regarded as an indulgence; as a matter of fact, some doctors are beginning to prescribe spa treatments for their patients. The cosmetology industry is at the forefront of new attitudes regarding mind/body awareness, relaxation techniques, nutrition, and spirituality. Now, men and women frequent the same salons, paying the same kind of attention to their hairstyles and appearance. Spas, which were considered the domain of rich old women for most of the 20th century, have become vacation spots of choice for men and women, young and old. And cosmetology, because of its stability, growth potential, and financial security, has been highly ranked in recent career surveys by *Money, Women's World,* and the U.S. Bureau of Labor Statistics.

Cosmetologists work in many different settings; they may rent a chair in a local hair styling salon or body-wrap spa guests at a tropical resort. "Day spas" are cropping up across the country, opening up jobs for cosmetologists with experience in massage, facials, nail care, and hydrotherapy. To compete, hair and nail salons are expanding to include additional rooms for face and body treatments. Fitness centers are also expanding their lines of service and are hiring massage therapists and spa attendants. New treatments, such as aromatherapy, and new products, such as herb-based, chemical-free cosmetics, require the industry to constantly change, adapting to trends and attitudes. But cosmetologists aren't limited to the spa and beauty salon. A variety of jobs are available in film and at recreational parks, cosmetology schools, funeral homes, and health clubs.

Cosmetologists who have finished training and have received a state license to practice usually start in entry-level positions in salons. These positions might include floor sweeping, shampooing clients' hair, making appointments, ordering supplies, and performing other tasks. Gradually, new cosmetologists take on more responsibilities and have more direct client contact, starting with simple cuts and styling. With more on-the-job experience while building a client base, they do more complicated cuts and styles, perms, and hair coloring.

Another popular alternative for cosmetologists is self-employment. Some freelance hair and makeup designers work with photographers, modeling agencies, film production companies, theaters, or television studios. Some open their own salons or rent a station in an established salon.

Because so many cosmetologists seek self-employment, there is a great deal of mobility within the industry. According to a 1999 survey conducted by the National Accrediting Commission of Cosmetology Arts and Sciences (NACCAS), one out of every three salon employees changed jobs in the last year. Approximately 25 percent of those who left salon establishments went into business for themselves, either as salon owners or booth renters.

There are a number of specialties within cosmetology. In hairstyling alone, cosmetologists can specialize in cuts, color, or perms. They may also become makeup artists, nail technicians, electrologists, image consultants, or developers and marketers of beauty products. According to the *Occupational Outlook Handbook,* there were 790,000 barbers, hairstylists, and cosmetologists, 40,000 manicurists and pedicurists, and 20,000 shampooers in 2000.

The cosmetology industry also includes people working in other career fields, such as health care (surgeons, dermatologists, surgical aides), the film industry (hair and makeup artists, costume designers, special effects artists), advertising, retail sales, fitness, and management. Magazine, newspaper, and Web publishing offer opportunities for full-time and consultant cosmetology experts. There are a variety of jobs available in the manufacturing of beauty and personal care products (such as cosmetics, hair care products, skin care products, and toiletries), including chemical scientists, technicians, packaging designers and engineers, advertising and marketing professionals, sales and distribution personnel, and production workers.

Check the yellow pages of your phone book under "Beauty Salons and Services" and you'll see how much the industry is growing—you're likely to find a long list of salons in your area. Day spas are also opening up across the country, and salons are expanding to include more spa services such as body wraps and massage. Hotels and resorts are adding salons, spas, and fitness centers to their facilities. The clientele of spas and salons has expanded to-include men. Many skin care lines carry products for men, and cosmetic surgery is gaining wider acceptance among both men and women.

Those in the cosmetology industry, through such professional organizations as NACCAS and the Cosmetology Advancement Foundation, are making efforts to educate people about the varied career options within the industry. Due to the growing number of salons and the mobility within the industry, these cosmetology associations are actively recruiting people to meet the industry's high demand for workers.

The U.S. Department of Labor projects average growth for all cosmetology occupations through 2010. The number of barbershops is declining, but trained barbers should not have difficulty finding jobs because of the lack of qualified applicants. The high rate of turnover in the cosmetology field and the continuing demand for services should create plenty of opportunities.

Each article in this book discusses a particular cosmetology industry occupation in detail. The information comes from Ferguson's *Encyclopedia of Careers and Vocational Guidance.* The **Overview** section is a brief introductory description of the duties and responsibilities of a person in the career. Oftentimes, a career may have a number of job titles. When this is the case, alternative career titles are presented in this section. The **History** section describes the history of the particular job as it relates to the overall development of its industry or field. The **Job** describes the primary and secondary duties of the job. **Requirements** discusses high school and postsecondary education and training requirements, any certification or licensing necessary, and any other personal requirements for success in the job. **Exploring** offers suggestions on how to gain some experience in or knowledge of the particular job before making a firm educational and financial commitment. The focus is on what can be done while still in high school (or in the early years of college) to gain a better understanding of the job. The **Employers** section gives an overview of typical places of employment for the job. **Starting Out** discusses the best ways to land that first job, be it through the college placement office, newspaper ads, or personal contact. The **Advancement** section describes what kind of career path to expect from the job and how to get there. **Earnings** lists salary ranges and describes the typical fringe benefits. The **Work Environment** section describes the typical surroundings and conditions of employment—whether indoors or outdoors, noisy or quiet, social or independent, and so on. Also discussed are typical hours worked, any seasonal fluctuations, and the stresses and strains of the job. The **Outlook** section summarizes the job in terms of the general economy and industry projections. For the most part, Outlook information is obtained from the Bureau of Labor Statistics and is supplemented by information taken from professional associations. Job growth terms follow those used in the *Occupational Outlook Handbook.* Growth described as "much faster than the average" means an increase of 36 percent or more. Growth described as "faster than the average" means an increase of 21 to 35 percent. Growth described as "about as fast as the average" means an increase of 10 to 20 percent. Growth described as "little change or more slowly than the average" means an increase of 0 to 9 percent. "Decline" means a decrease of 1 percent or more.

Each article ends with **For More Information,** which lists organizations that can provide career information on training, education, internships, scholarships, and job placement.

Aromatherapists

Overview

Aromatherapists are health care specialists who use a deep understanding of the principles of aromatherapy to help their clients live healthier, more satisfying lives. Aromatherapy is the science and art of using essential plant oils to promote health. Essential oils are highly concentrated substances that give plants their fragrance. These substances are extracted from various parts of aromatic plants—roots, woods, seeds, fruits, leaves, and flowers, among others. Only about 5 percent of all types of plants are used for their essential oils.

Since the early 20th century, the professions of cosmetology, medicine, and psychology have rediscovered the healing powers of essential oils that were known to earlier civilizations. Scientific studies show that inhaling the fragrance of certain essential oils has physiological and psychological effects on the brain. Aromatherapists study the oils and their effects on individuals. They use this knowledge to help improve their clients' quality of life.

Most aromatherapists are licensed in other areas of health care or body care. They study and practice aromatherapy as a healing modality that is supplementary to the profession in which they are licensed. Among these licensed professionals are beauticians, chiropractors, cosmeticians, massage therapists, medical doctors, naturopathic doctors, nurse practitioners, and nurses. A few individuals who specialize in aromatherapy work as chemists, educators, or authors. A very few grow plants for the distillation of essential oils, become consultants, or start their own lines of aromatherapy products.

History

Humanity's use of fragrance probably began long before recorded history. Anthropologists think that primitive people burned gums and resin as incense. Throughout history, civilizations have used essential oils for many purposes—including healing. As an art and science, aromatherapy finds its roots in ancient cultures, dating back 4,000 to 5,000 years. Early Egyptians are often credited with being the first to make an art of the use of essential oils. They used myrrh and frankincense (fragrant resins from trees) in their daily rituals. However, other early cultures also used essential oils. In ancient Africa, people discovered that certain plants provided protection from the sun when they were rubbed on the skin. Chinese, Indian, Persian, and other African cultures used plant oils for incense burning, cooking, cosmetics, mummifying, bathing, perfumery, meditating, and healing.

In the spas of ancient Rome, oils were used in public baths and were applied during massages. The knowledge of oils went along with the spread of Roman culture. Europeans used oils during medieval times to fight disease. During the Middle Ages, the appearance of chemistry and the improvement of distillation helped simplify the process of extracting essential oils from plants. This opened the door to oil trading, which spread the new practices to more people and places.

Until the 19th century, when science began to introduce other medicines, Europeans used essential oils both as perfumes and for medicinal purposes. With the growth of newer medical practices, doctors began to choose modern medicine over the tradition of oils. It was not until the 20th century that several individuals "rediscovered" the healing power of essential oils. Once again the use of oils was integrated into Western culture.

In 1928, the French perfumer and chemist, René-Maurice Gattefossé, experienced the healing power of essential oils. When he severely burned his hand, he stuck it into the nearest liquid, which happened to be lavender oil. He was surprised how quickly the hand healed. His experience caused him to become interested in the therapeutic use of essential oils. It was Gattefossé who coined the term aromatherapy.

Dr. Jean Valnet, a French physician, was the first to reintegrate essential oils into Western medical practice. Dr. Valnet served as an army surgeon during World War II. Inspired by the work of Gattefossé, he used essential oils to treat the soldiers' burns and wounds. He also successfully treated psychiatric problems with fragrances. Marguerite Maury, an Austrian biochemist, was also influenced by the work of Gattefossé. She integrated the use of essential oils into cosmetics.

In 1977, Robert Tisserand, an expert in aromatherapy, wrote *The Art of Aromatherapy.* Tisserand was strongly influenced by the work of both Gattefossé and Valnet. His book caught the interest of the American public and made a major contribution to the growth of aromatherapy in this country.

The Western world has rediscovered the uses of essential oils and fragrances through the work of people such as Valnet, Maury, and Tisserand. In France, aromatherapy is practiced by medical doctors. Conventional and alternative medicine practitioners in England, Australia, Sweden, Japan, the United States, and other parts of the world are recognizing and utilizing the healing power of essential oils. The world is reawakening to the healing and life-enhancing capabilities of aromatherapy.

The Job

Whether aromatherapists work primarily as beauticians, chiropractors, massage therapists, or doctors, they must possess a strong working knowledge of aromatherapy as a science and an art. They need to understand the components and healing benefits of many essential oils. The quality of essential oils varies greatly depending on the plant, where it is grown, the conditions under which it is grown, and other factors. As a result, aromatherapists must be very careful about choosing the sources from which their oils come. Pure, high-quality, therapeutic grade oils are essential to good aromatherapy. Aromatherapists must even know the differences between the oils of different species of the same plant. Essential oils are very powerful because of their high concentration. It may take well over 100 pounds of plant material to produce just one pound of essential oil.

Because of the powerful concentration of essential oils, aromatherapists use great care in diluting them and in adding them to carriers. Carriers are most often high-quality vegetable oils, such as almond, olive, or sesame. Unlike essential oils, carrier oils are fixed, rather than volatile. A small amount of an essential oil is blended into the carrier oil, which "carries" it across the body. Aromatherapists are especially careful when the oils are to be applied to a client's skin or put into a bath. In addition, aromatherapists must know how different essential oils work together because they combine oils to achieve certain results.

Aromatherapists need to know much more than what oils to use. They use the essential oils in three types of aromatherapy: cosmetic, massage, and olfactory. Aromatherapists have to know the differences among the types of therapy. They must decide which type or combination of types to use in a particular situation, and they must be skilled in each type.

Aromatherapists must know how the body, mind, and emotions work together. For example, a client who complains of muscle tension may need physical relief. A massage with relaxing oils that the skin soaks in will relax the client. However, aromatherapists are able to take this treatment a step further. They consider the underlying causes of the condition. Why is the client feeling tense? Is it stress? Anxiety? Strong emotion? Massage therapists who are trained in aromatherapy may inquire about the client's life in order to pinpoint the source of the tension. Once the source is identified, aromatherapists utilize specific oils to produce a certain emotional effect in the client. When the scents of these oils are inhaled, they create a response within the entire body. The oils may be added to a bath or a compress that is applied to the body. A compress is a towel soaked in water that has a bit of an essential oil added to it. An aroma may take the client back to happier times, as a reminder of warmth, comfort, and contentment.

An aromatherapist's client may have skin problems due to stress. The aromatherapist may use certain essential oils to help both the skin condition on the surface and the underlying emotional source of the problem. This might be accomplished through olfactory aromatherapy— the inhalation of the oil vapors.

In a hospital, nursing home, or hospice setting, an aromatherapist might choose essential oils that help relieve stress. In England, hospital nursing staffs utilize essential oil massage. This type of therapy has been shown to relieve pain and induce sleep. Essential oil massage has proven effective in relieving the stress that patients experience with general illness, surgery, terminal cancer, and AIDS. Aromatherapists emphasize that these treatments are supplementary and enhancing to medical care—they do not replace medical treatment.

No two clients' problems are the same, and neither are the remedies for those problems. Each client must be treated as an individual. During the first visit, aromatherapists usually take a careful client history. Aromatherapists must listen carefully for both those things their clients say and for those important things they don't say. Aromatherapists need to know if a client is taking any medicine or using any natural healing substances, such as herbs. They must understand the properties of the essential oils and how they might interact with any other treatment the client is using. Next, they use the information gathered from the client interview to determine the proper essential oils and the appropriate amounts to blend to serve the client's particular needs.

Aromatherapists are employed in a number of different work environments. Those connected to the beauty industry may work in salons, spas, or hotel resorts. They incorporate aromatherapy into facial care, body care, and hair care. In the health care field, many professionals are turning to alternative approaches to care, and some conventional medical practitioners are beginning to implement more holistic approaches. As a result, a growing number of aromatherapists work in the offices of other health care specialists where their aromatherapy treatments complement the other therapies used. Aromatherapists often give seminars, teach, or serve as consultants. Some who become experts on essential oils buy farms to grow plants for the oils, create their own lines of aromatherapy products, or sell essential oils to other aromatherapists.

Requirements

HIGH SCHOOL

If you are interested in working with aromatherapy, begin in high school by building up your knowledge of the human body's systems. Biology, anatomy, and physiology will help lay the foundation for a career in aromatherapy. Chemistry courses will familiarize you with laboratory procedures. Aromatherapists need to have an understanding of mixtures and the care involved in using powerful essential oils. Chemistry can help you gain the experience you need to handle delicate or volatile substances. It will also familiarize you with the properties of natural compounds.

Keep in mind that the majority of aromatherapists are self-employed. Math, business, and computer courses will help you develop the skills you need to be successful at running a business.

Aromatherapists also need good communication and interpersonal skills to be sensitive to their clients. English, speech, and psychology classes can help you sharpen your ability to interact constructively with other people.

Eva-Marie Lind is an aromatherapist, author, and former Dean of the Aromatherapy Department of the Australasian College of Herbal Studies in Lake Oswego, Oregon. She has worked in the field of aromatherapy for over 15 years. According to Lind, "Education is the key to good aromatherapy. There is so much to learn, and it takes real dedication to study."

POSTSECONDARY TRAINING

In 1999 the National Association for Holistic Aromatherapy (NAHA) established criteria for aromatherapy education that have been voluntarily adopted by a number of schools and education programs. NAHA guidelines recommend that aromatherapy education include courses on topics such as the history of aromatherapy, physiology, production of essential oils, botany, chemistry, safety and methods of application, and business planning.

While the NAHA provides a listing of schools complying with its guidelines, there are also other schools, seminars, and distance learning courses that offer training in aromatherapy. Be aware, however, that the quality of programs can vary. Take the time to call the schools or organizations that interest you. Ask how their programs are set up. For correspondence courses (or distance courses), ask if you will be able to talk to a teacher. How will you be evaluated? Are there tests? How are the tests taken and graded? Try to talk with current students. Ask how they are treated and what they learn. Ask what you receive when you graduate from the program. Will you receive help with job placement? Access to insurance programs? Other benefits? Depending on the program you pick, the length of study ranges from short workshops to four-year college courses. Vocational schools, major universities, and naturopathic colleges are increasingly offering training in aromatherapy.

Most aromatherapists are also professionals in other fields. Consider whether you would want to combine aromatherapy with a "base" profession, such as chiropractic, massage therapy, nursing, or some other field into which you might incorporate it. These base fields require additional education and certification as well as licensing. If you decide to add aromatherapy to another profession, learn the requirements for certification or licensing that apply to that profession. Adding aromatherapy to another profession requires a comprehensive understanding of both fields from a scientific standpoint.

CERTIFICATION OR LICENSING

There are presently no certification or licensing requirements for aromatherapy in the United States. Aromatherapy is growing rapidly, and it is likely that these requirements will be established soon. Since aromatherapy is practiced by such a variety of professionals, developing standards is particularly complex. Nevertheless, professionals throughout the industry are working toward this goal. If you choose to study aromatherapy, you will need to keep up on these changes.

If you choose to combine aromatherapy with another profession, you must meet the national and local requirements for that field in addition to aromatherapy requirements.

OTHER REQUIREMENTS

According to Eva-Marie Lind, "Aromatherapy demands love and passion at its roots. You need to honor, respect, and celebrate the beauty of this field." You must also enjoy disseminating knowledge because clients often have many questions. More practically, it takes a good nose and a certain sensitivity to successfully treat clients through aromatherapy. It takes good listening skills and immense creativity to understand each client's personal issues and decide on the best means of administering a treatment. Which essential oils or combination of oils should you choose? Should you use a bath, a compress, a massage, or inhalation? What parts of the body are the best avenues for delivering the remedy?

Aromatherapists must be good self-teachers who are interested in continuing education. This is a relatively new field that is developing and changing rapidly. To stay competitive and successful, you need to keep up with the changing trends, products, and technologies that affect the field. Like most healing professions, aromatherapy is a lifelong education process for the practitioner.

Exploring

There are many ways to explore the field of aromatherapy to see if it is for you. For one, there are many books and specialized periodicals available on the subject. Get a glimpse of the types of knowledge you need for the field. Find out whether it is too scientific or not scientific enough.

Look in your local library for books and magazines that show you what a typical student of aromatherapy might be learning.

Visit health food stores. The staff members of health food stores are often very helpful. Most have books, magazines, and newspapers about many kinds of alternative health care, including aromatherapy. Ask about essential oils, and ask for the names of aromatherapists in the area. Find out if there are garden clubs that you can join—particularly ones that specialize in herbs. Consider taking up cooking. This could give you practice in selecting herbs and seasonings and blending them to create different aromas and flavors.

Contact local and national professional organizations. Some offer student memberships or free seminars. Check out their Web sites. They have a lot of valuable information and good links to other alternative health care sites. Join online forums and discussion groups where you can communicate with professionals from all over the country and the world. Some distance learning courses are open to students of all ages.

If you find you have a real interest in aromatherapy, another way to explore the field is to seek a mentor—a professional in the field who is willing to help you learn. Tell everyone you know that you are interested in aromatherapy. Someone is bound to have a connection with someone you could call for an informational interview. Perhaps you could spend a day "shadowing" an aromatherapist to see what the work is like. If you are unable to find an aromatherapy specialist, you could call spas and salons in search of professionals who use aromatherapy in their work. Perhaps some would be willing to speak to you about their day-to-day work. Make an appointment and experience an aromatherapy treatment. Taking it a step further, you could explore the possibility of getting a part-time job at an establishment that employs aromatherapists.

Employers

Most aromatherapists are self-employed. They run their own small businesses and build their own clientele. Some set up their own offices, but many build their businesses by working in the offices of other professionals and giving aromatherapy treatments as supplements to the treatments provided by the resident professionals. Many different kinds of employers are looking for skilled aromatherapists. In the cosmetic industry, beauticians, cosmeticians, and massage therapists employ aromatherapists to give treatments that complement their own. Spas, athletic clubs, resorts, and cruise ships may hire aromatherapists on a full-time basis. These types of employment may be temporary or seasonal.

In the health care industry, chiropractors, acupuncturists, and other alternative therapy practitioners and clinics may offer aromatherapy in addition to their basic services. Hospitals, nursing homes, hospice centers, and other medical establishments are beginning to recognize the physiological and psychological benefits of aromatherapy for their patients.

Starting Out

Because the practice of aromatherapy may be incorporated into numerous other professions, there are many ways to enter the field. How you enter depends on how you want to use aromatherapy. Is your interest in massage therapy, skin care, or hair care? Do you want to be a nurse, doctor, acupuncturist, or chiropractor? Are you interested in becoming an instructor or writer? Once you are certified in another area, you need to search for clinics, salons, spas, and other establishments that are looking for professionals who use aromatherapy in their treatments. School career services are also ways to find work. Classified ads in newspapers and trade magazines list positions in the related fields.

Networking can be an important source of job opportunities. Networking is simply getting to know others and exchanging ideas with them. Go to association meetings and conventions. Talk to people in the field. Job openings are often posted at such gatherings.

Advancement

Aromatherapists can advance to many different levels, depending on their goals, ambitions, aspirations, and willingness to work. Those who are self-employed can increase their clientele, and open their own offices or even a salon. Those who are employed at a spa or salon could become a department director or the director of the entire spa or salon. They might start a private practice or open a spa or salon.

As their skills and knowledge grow, aromatherapists may be sought after to teach and train other aromatherapists in seminars or at schools that offer aromatherapy programs or courses. Others become consultants or write books and articles. A few start their own aromatherapy product lines of esthetic or therapeutic products. Some may become involved in growing the plants that are the sources of essential oils. Still others work in distilling, analyzing, or blending the oils.

This is such a new field growing so rapidly that the potential for advancement is enormous. The field has so many facets that the directions for growth are as great as your imagination and determination. Geraldine Zelinsky, the public relations representative of the National Association for Holistic Aromatherapists, says, "If you are self-motivated, creative, and have a talent for any aspect of aromatherapy, the sky is the limit. It is what you make it."

Earnings

Since aromatherapists work in such a variety of settings, and aromatherapy is often a supplementary therapy added to other professional training, it is particularly difficult to make statements about average earnings in the field. Government agencies do not yet have wage statistics for the field. The national professional associations have not yet developed surveys of their members that give reliable information.

For those who are self-employed in any profession, earnings depend on the amount of time they work and the amount they charge per hour. Experienced professional aromatherapists estimate that hourly rates can range from $25 to $65 for beginning aromatherapists and instructors. Rates increase with experience to between $75 and $100 per hour. Based on those rates, a beginning aromatherapist who charged $25 an hour and averaged 10 appointments per week would earn around $13,000. Established aromatherapists who have a solid client base report earning $25,000 to $45,000.

The hourly rate an aromatherapist charges depends on his or her level of expertise, the type of clientele served, and even the area of the country. In many of the larger cities and much of the West Coast, people are already more aware and accepting of alternative health therapies. In those areas, higher hourly rates will be more accepted. Where such therapies are practically unknown, lower rates will apply. Another consideration for the self-employed is that they must provide their own insurance and retirement plans and pay for their supplies and other business expenses.

An aromatherapist with determination, creativity, and initiative can find jobs that pay well. Some who run exclusive spas or develop their own lines of aromatherapy products are reported to earn $70,000 to $80,000 or more.

Aromatherapists who are primarily employed in other professions, such as massage therapists, chiropractors, cosmetologists, and nurses, can expect to make the salaries that are average for their profession. Those professionals who use aromatherapy as a supportive therapy to their primary profession tend to have higher incomes than those who specialize in aromatherapy. The addition of aromatherapy to their profession will probably enhance their clients' and their own satisfaction, but it may not increase their income.

Work Environment

Aromatherapists work in a service-oriented environment, in which the main duty involves understanding and helping their clients. The surroundings are usually clean, peaceful, and pleasant. They work with very potent substances (strong essential oils), but most aromatherapists love the scents and the experience of the oils. They often spend a great deal of time on their feet. They sometimes work long or inconsistent hours, such as weekends and evenings, to accommodate their clients' needs.

Aromatherapists are people-oriented. They work with people and must be able to work well both individually and on teams. Those who are self-employed must be highly motivated and able to work alone. Aromatherapists who work in clinics, spas, hospitals, resorts, and other locations need to be good team players.

Outlook

Aromatherapy has been growing very rapidly and is just beginning to gather steam in the United States. Opportunities are increasing rapidly as public awareness of alternative therapies is increasing.

The status of aromatherapy in European and other countries may provide a glimpse of the future of the field in the United States. In Great Britain and France, for example, more doctors have embraced aromatherapy, and these services are covered by major health plans. If the United States follows this lead, new doors will open in this field. In general, the outlook is very good for aromatherapy because of an overwhelming increase in public awareness and interest.

For More Information

The National Association for Holistic Aromatherapy (NAHA) is one of the oldest and largest nonprofit educational organizations in the United States. It is dedicated to the development of high standards of aromatherapy teaching and practice. In 1999 the NAHA developed Guidelines for Professional Aromatherapy Training. See the Web site for a listing of schools in compliance with these guidelines.

THE NATIONAL ASSOCIATION FOR HOLISTIC AROMATHERAPY (NAHA)
4509 Interlake Avenue North, Suite 233
Seattle, WA 98103-6773
Tel: 888-ASK-NAHA
Email: info@naha.org
Web: http://www.naha.org

For information regarding state regulations for massage therapists and general information on therapeutic massage, contact:
AMERICAN MASSAGE THERAPY ASSOCIATION
820 Davis Street, Suite 100
Evanston, IL 60201-4444
Tel: 847-864-0123
Web: http://www.amtamassage.org

For comprehensive Internet information on alternative and conventional health care and extensive links, visit:
HEALTHWORLDONLINE
Web: http://www.healthy.net

Barbers

Overview

Barbers shampoo, cut, trim, and style hair and shave, trim, and shape beards. While barbers are formally trained to perform other services such as coloring and perming hair, most barbers in barbershops do not offer these services. Barbers may also call themselves *barber-stylists*, and a few may even refer to themselves as *tonsorial artists*, an old-fashioned term that is derived from a Latin word meaning "to shear."

Quick Facts

School Subjects
  Business
  Health
Personal Skills
  Artistic
  Mechanical/manipulative
Work Environment
  Primarily indoors
  Primarily one location
Minimum Education Level
  Some postsecondary training
Salary Range
  $12,030 to $17,740 to $33,040+
Certification or Licensing
  Required
Outlook
  Decline

History

Barbering boasts a long and rich history. The word barber is derived from the Latin word *barba*, meaning beard. Archeologists tell us that the cave dwellers of 20,000 years ago tweezed their whiskers with clam shells. There are several Biblical references that reflect the Egyptian preoccupation with facial hair and shaving. As early as 500 BC, barbers began establishing themselves in Greece, and their sidewalk shops became gathering places for discussions of sports, philosophy, politics, and gossip. Of course, not everyone appreciated the talkative barber: when King Archelaus, who ruled Macedon from 413 to 399 BC, was asked by his barber how he wanted his hair cut, he replied, "In silence." Greek barbers also served as dietitians as well as setting broken bones, giving enemas, bloodletting, and performing minor surgeries.

During the Dark Ages, barbers began to be known as barber-surgeons. They performed medical procedures such as bloodletting, tooth extraction, and minor surgeries. In England, during the reign of Henry VIII, from 1509 to 1547, the two professions were separated by an act forbidding barber-surgeons to perform any surgical procedures except tooth extractions and bloodletting. In 1745, the final split between barbers and surgeons occurred under an act of George II. Following this act, the barber profession gradually declined to the status of wigmakers, as wigs became the rage during the 18th century. By the end of the 1700s, nearly all barbers, except those in remote areas, had ceased practicing surgical or dental procedures. Bloodletting was not abandoned as a practice until the 19th century, long after George Washington's personal physician had literally bled him to death while attempting to cure a windpipe infection.

The period between the Civil War and World War II was truly the heyday of the American barbershop. The familiar red and white pole—symbolizing the bandages used on a bleeding patient—was a welcoming sight to a weary traveler. In a short time, the dirty, scruffy, smelly stranger would be transformed into a bathed, shaved, perfumed, and shorn gentleman. His boots would be shined, his pants would be pressed, and he may even have been offered a cigar and a mug of beer. During his grooming session, he was sure to be informed of local employment opportunities and where he might find room and board. Many barbershops were open 12 hours a day and even early Sunday morning, when, for a few nickels, a man could get his face lathered and shaved before church. As in ancient Greece and Rome, barbershops were places of gossip, socializing, and often live music (the famous "barbershop quartet" style of singing in four-part harmony).

Today, barbershops—which once outnumbered saloons in many towns—are dwindling as beauty salons and spas flourish. With the gender line steadily eroding in matters of cosmetology, many men are turning to full-service shops for manicures and special hairstyles and procedures. However, most barbers have a loyal clientele, which steadily increases the longer a barber is in business. According to an executive of a national association for barbers, the average barber today has been on the job for 27.1 years.

Fashion and imitation have always played a significant role in the evolution of hairstyles. In earlier times, much like today, styles that met with disapproval among one generation became the accepted styles for the next. Barbers have observed various trends in business based on the styles of the celebrities of the day. For example, many barbers saw business slow down gradually following the advent of Beatlemania. In the 1980s, the movie *Top Gun* spurred a renewed popularity of the short haircut. Today, Michael Jordan is credited by many for a surge in youngsters and men seeking very short haircuts that require frequent trimming.

The Job

Most barbers in barbershops focus primarily on the basics of men's grooming needs: hair cutting and trimming, shampooing, styling, and beard and mustache trimming and shaping. Many include a brief facial, scalp, and/or neck massage. While some barbers do perform other services, such as tinting or bleaching, most find that few of their customers seek such services, and those that do are more likely to head for a full-service salon. Shaving is far less common in barbershops today than it once was. The safety razor has made shaving at home a relatively quick and easy task, and the art of the straight-edge shave is little more than a relic of tonsorial history.

Most customers who frequent barbershops are men, but some women—particularly those with short hair—do patronize barbers. Likewise, most barbers are men, but the field includes some female barbers as well.

The equipment barbers utilize—clippers, razors, shears, combs, brushes, and so forth—must be kept in antiseptic condition. Often barbers must supply their own equipment. Barbers who operate their own shops must handle the details of answering phones and setting appointments, ordering supplies and paying bills, maintaining equipment, and keeping records. If they employ other barbers, they are responsible for the hiring and performance of their staff as well. Barbershops range from one-person operations to larger shops with many chairs and operators.

Requirements

HIGH SCHOOL
Many states require that barbers be high school graduates, although a few states require only an eighth-grade education. High school students considering a career as a barber might find it helpful to take courses in health and business. Involvement in theater can provide you with opportunities to practice working on hair and attempting to create different styles as well as give you the opportunity to develop "people skills" you will need later when dealing with the public.

POSTSECONDARY TRAINING

Generally, a barber must complete a certain number of hours of barber school (ranging from 1,000 to 2,000 hours, depending on the state). Most states offer programs that include classroom work, demonstrations, and hands-on work and can be completed in 10 to 24 months. The barber must then pass an examination that includes a written test (and sometimes an oral test) and a practical examination to demonstrate that skills are mastered. A health certificate must also be obtained. In selecting a barber school, a student should be sure the school meets (and preferably exceeds) the state's requirements for licensing. Some schools have waiting lists, so it may be prudent to apply early.

At one time, a one- to two-year apprenticeship was required in many states before a barber was "full-fledged." This practice is becoming less common as formal training is increasingly emphasized. In a few rural states, an apprenticeship can take the place of formal education, but this is an uncommon and difficult way to acquire sufficient skill and knowledge.

CERTIFICATION OR LICENSING

All barbers must be licensed to practice in the state in which they work, although the requirements vary from state to state. Some states have licensing reciprocity agreements that enable barbers to practice in another state without being retested. Some states require that barbers be at least 18 years old in order to be licensed.

Unions were once prevalent among barbers, but they are becoming less common, especially in rural areas. Today there are fewer barbers in the workforce than there were decades ago, and a large percentage of them are self-employed. The National Cosmetology Association lists the United Food and Commercial Workers International Union as the principal union that organizes barbers.

OTHER REQUIREMENTS

Barbering requires good finger dexterity and stamina, since barbers are required to be on their feet most of the day (although work environments can often be adapted to accommodate workers with disabilities or special needs). Barbers should themselves be neat and well-groomed because they work in close proximity to their customers. Tact and patience are important characteristics, as is being a good listener. The ability to easily carry on light conversation is important as well. Roy Bollhoffer, owner of Roy's Barbershop in Highland Park, Illinois, stresses the importance of being a "people person." Says Bollhoffer about being a barber, "If you don't like people, you're in trouble." Bollhoffer has owned his barbershop for 34 years; he bought it from a barber who started his business just after World War I. Nearly all of Bollhoffer's customers have been with him for many years, and quite a few have patronized his shop for even longer than the 34 years Bollhoffer has been there. Like many barbers, Bollhoffer finds that once customers find a barber they like, they stick with him or her until they die or move, or until the barber retires.

To be successful, barbers must understand the importance their customers place on their appearances and seriously strive to provide a look that pleases their customers. An executive in a national association for barbers notes, "You're in the business of making people happy." Barbers should have a sense of form and style in order to determine what looks would be most flattering for individual customers. A barber must also recognize when a style desired by a customer isn't suited to the customer's features or hair type in order to avoid customer dissatisfaction. These situations require firmness and diplomacy.

Exploring

If you are interested in this career, try finding part-time employment in a barbershop or beauty salon to gain exposure to the nature of the work and the working conditions. Another avenue of exploration might be to call a barber school and ask for an opportunity to tour the facilities, observe classes, and question instructors. Of course, nothing compares to talking to someone with firsthand experience; a chat with a local barber is a sure and easy way to obtain helpful and informative feedback.

Employers

A barber's domain is almost exclusively the barbershop. While some barbers may find work in a full-service styling salon, most of these businesses are seeking stylists with broader training and experience. Most barbers are self-employed, either owning their own shops or renting a chair at a barbershop. In the days before beauty salons were so prevalent—and before men frequented them—nearly all men had their hair cut by barbers. Today, these men still comprise a significant portion of barbershops' clienteles, so opportunities for barbers may be better in areas with a higher concentration of older men. Some barbers are employed as teachers/trainers at barber schools, and some may also serve as inspectors for the State Board of Barber Examiners.

Starting Out

In most states, the best way (and often the only way) to enter the field of barbering is to graduate from a barber school that meets the state's requirements for licensing and to pass the state's licensing examination. Nearly all barber schools assist graduates with the process of finding employment opportunities. As barbershops are few in many areas, calling or visiting a barbershop is an excellent way to find employment. In some areas, there may be barbering unions that may be helpful in one's job search. While a part-time job in a barbershop or beauty shop can be helpful in determining one's level of interest in the field, satisfying the graduation requirements of an accredited barber school and becoming licensed is usually the only way to enter this occupation.

Advancement

The most common form of advancement in the barbering profession is owning one's own shop. This requires business experience and skill as well as proficiency in the barbering profession, and of course start-up requires capital outlay. Those who are successful as owners do reap higher earnings than barbers who rent a booth in a shop or are paid on a commission basis. Some even go on to own a chain of barbershops. In larger barbershops, there may be opportunities for management, but these are relatively rare. The longer a barber is on the job, though, the larger the clientele (and thus the security and income) becomes.

Barbers can increase their opportunities for advancement by becoming licensed as cosmetologists and working in larger beauty shops that provide more complicated, varied, and advanced services. Opportunities for management or specializing in certain services are increasingly plentiful in full-service salons. Many states require a separate license for cosmetology, but often barbering training can be applied toward a cosmetology license. In a few states, the two licenses are combined into one hair styling license.

Related career opportunities may exist if a barber wishes to become an instructor at a barber school or an inspector for the State Board of Barber Examiners.

Earnings

Incomes can vary widely depending on a barber's experience, the location of the shop, the number of hours worked, tipping habits of the clientele, and whether or not a barber owns the business. The personality and initiative of a barber also impact the ability to draw a loyal following. The U.S. Department of Labor reports the median annual income for full-time, salaried barbers, including tips, as $17,740 in 2000. The highest paid 10 percent earned more than $33,040 per year, while the lowest paid 10 percent earned less than $12,030 annually. Many established barbers and barber/owners earn incomes that well exceed the median.

One of the most frequently cited downsides to being a barber is a lack of benefits, particularly where there are no unions. Many barbers cannot get group insurance, and the cost of individual policies can be high. Also, since most barbers are either self-employed or working for small shops, benefits such as retirement plans, paid vacations, sick days, and so forth are often the exception to the rule.

Work Environment

Barbers generally enjoy pleasant work surroundings. The barbershop environment is usually friendly, clean, and comfortable. Many barbers can set their own hours, and although many work Saturdays, they typically take Sundays and weeknights off. Of course, this depends largely on the schedules of their clientele; barbers whose clientele consists mostly of retirees rarely find the need to work evenings. Stress levels and job pressures are lower than is the case with most jobs. Established barbers enjoy a unique security in that their clients are usually very loyal and always need haircuts. Most barbers don't share the fears of layoffs and other job insecurities common to other professions. Compared to their cosmetologist counterparts, barbers are exposed to fewer hair and nail chemicals, which also enhances the work environment. Most barbers have been on the job for many years, and there is clearly a great deal of pride and job enjoyment among barbers. This is a good profession for those who enjoy the company of other people.

Outlook

As the beauty industry has flourished, the number of old-fashioned barbershops has waned. More and more, men have turned to styling salons rather than barbershops to have their styling and grooming needs met. In addition, only a small number of cosmetology school graduates are getting barbering licenses. The U.S. Department of Labor predicts a decline in the employment of barbers through 2010.

Many job openings will result from the need to replace retired workers. And since there are few qualified candidates, those entering the field may find good opportunities, depending on their location. Says Roy Bollhoffer, "I had another barber here with me for 27 years, but he retired. I'd love to find another barber to bring in, but there is a serious shortage of barbers now. And there will always be people who want to go to a barber. I've made a very nice living here." In all likelihood, the outlook for this profession will be different for various cities, states, and regions of the country.

For More Information

For information about the profession as well as a list of licensed training schools, contact:
NATIONAL ACCREDITING COMMISSION OF COSMETOLOGY ARTS AND SCIENCES
4401 Ford Avenue, Suite 1300
Alexandria, VA 22302-1432
Tel: 703-600-7600
Web: http://www.naccas.org

To read about hair myths and tips and access a listing of hair and beauty schools, visit the following Web site:
HAIR INTERNATIONAL
Web: http://www.heaven-earth.com

Color Analysts and Image Consultants

Overview

Color analysts assess their clients' coloring, including skin tone and hair and eye color, and teach them how to use their most flattering colors in clothing and makeup. *Image consultants* usually work with people in business, helping them present themselves in a professional manner.

Color and image consultants offer programs for individual women or men, for professional or social organizations, or for all the employees of one company. Some work with retailers, teaching salespersons about color and style and presenting in-store workshops.

History

In their book, *Color Me Beautiful's Looking Your Best,* Mary Spillane and Christine Sherlock cite a study by Albert Mehrabian. He found that the impression we make on others is made up of 55 percent appearance and behavior, 38 percent speech, and only 7 percent what we say. These figures clearly show the importance of presenting yourself well in business, social, and other settings. Color analysts and image consultants have been around for some time, but their work is constantly evolving. Because our society is increasingly mobile, and we change jobs more often than our parents did, we are constantly establishing ourselves with new groups. In addition, television has increased our awareness of appearance and what it tells us about the individual. Projecting a positive image through our appearance and behavior helps us gain acceptance from social and business contacts, fit into the workplace, and meet the public.

In 1980, with publication of Carole Jackson's book, *Color Me Beautiful,* many people, especially women, began to think of what they purchased and wore in a different way. No longer willing to accept whatever fashion decreed, they wanted colors and styles that enhanced their individual appearance. By the time more than 20 million people had read this *New York Times* bestseller, clothing manufacturers, cosmetic companies, and retailers felt the impact of the new consumer demand.

In the meantime, other businesses were dealing with their increased need for employees with technological backgrounds. Such employees often were totally involved in the technical aspects of their work and unconcerned about the impression they made on coworkers, clients, and the general public. Many companies began to provide training to help employees project better images, increasing the demand for image consultants.

The Job

Most color and image consultants are entrepreneurs, meaning that they own and manage their businesses and assume all the risks. They may work with individuals, groups, or both. Christine Sherlock, director of training and communications for Color Me Beautiful, reports that her firm trains color analysts in color and its use in wardrobe and makeup. Those who wish to become image consultants take additional training so they can help clients work on their overall appearance and grooming, as well as improve their voices, body language, and etiquette. Consultants also may learn to coach clients on dealing with the public and the media.

Susan Fignar, president of S. Fignar & Associates, Inc., is a corporate image trainer and consultant who has been quoted in *Cosmopolitan,* the *Wall Street Journal,* and the *Chicago Tribune.* She works with some of the country's largest corporations and offers a variety of corporate programs and interactive workshops. Fignar says she provides training that helps people bring out their best personal and professional presence. Like other entrepreneurs, her business requires constant sales and marketing to obtain clients.

Fignar's training sessions deal with such topics as making a good first impression, everyday etiquette, developing self-esteem and confidence, verbal communication, body language and facial expression, overall appearance, and appropriate dress for every occasion. She notices an increasing demand for her services in dress code consulting and training sessions on business casual dress.

Sherlock says consultants get satisfaction from helping others look better and feel good about themselves. "When a consultant helps a client with her wardrobe," she says, "the client not only saves money; she uses 100 percent of her wardrobe and no longer complains she has nothing to wear."

Requirements

HIGH SCHOOL
If you are interested in this work, you will benefit from taking classes and being involved in activities that develop your ability to communicate and increase your understanding of visual effects. Helpful classes to take include English, speech, and drama. Activities to consider participating in include drama clubs and debate teams. In drama club you may have the opportunity to help apply makeup, select wardrobes, and learn about the emotional impact appearances can have. Art classes are also helpful to take, especially classes that teach color theory. Since many people in this line of work are entrepreneurs, consider taking any business, bookkeeping, or accounting classes that will give you the skills to run your own business.

Any part-time job working with the public is valuable. You can gain excellent experience from selling clothing or cosmetics in department stores, from working in beauty salons or spas, or from working as a waitperson. Volunteer work that involves working with people will also help you hone your people skills.

POSTSECONDARY TRAINING
There are no formal, standardized training programs for color analysts and image consultants. In general, Susan Fignar recommends attending seminars or classes on color, psychology, training methods, and communications. She adds that a degree in liberal arts, with a major in education, is a plus for those working at the corporate level.

Color Me Beautiful has trainers who travel throughout the country. They offer people who wish to become consultants basic classes in skin care, makeup, and color analysis and advanced classes in such subjects as theory of style and presentation. Most classes take one or two days for a single topic; most working consultants take at least one new class each year.

If you get to know a color analyst or image consultant personally, you may be able to arrange an informal internship of your own. Some people begin their careers in this field by working as apprentices to other consultants. Color Me Beautiful accepts a two-month apprenticeship with an approved consultant.

CERTIFICATION OR LICENSING
Various training programs offer certificates to students once they have completed course work. The Association of Image Consultants International (AICI) provides a listing of such organizations on its Web site. The AICI recommends researching programs or training sessions, considering such factors as cost, length of study, subject areas covered, and refund policies. Color and image consultants require no licensing.

OTHER REQUIREMENTS
Christine Sherlock recommends this field for those who like to work with and help other people and says an interest in fashion and style are also obviously very helpful. A general flair for art and design would prove useful. Analysts and consultants should be friendly, outgoing, supportive of others, able to offer constructive feedback, and open to change. There are few disabilities that would prevent an individual from doing this work.

Susan Fignar believes experience in the business world, especially in management and public contact, is essential for corporate consulting. She says that corporate consultants must be mature, poised, and professional to have credibility, and that people are usually between the ages of 33 and 40 when they enter this field.

Exploring

One way to explore this career is to arrange for a personal visit to a consultant. The Association of Image Consultants International, for example, offers lists of qualified consultants throughout the country (see the end of this article for contact information).

There are several books you can read to learn more about color and image consulting. Christine Sherlock recommends *Color Me Beautiful* by Carole Jackson (Ballantine Books, 1987), *Color Me Beautiful's Looking Your Best: Color, Makeup, and Style* by Mary Spillane and Christine Sherlock (Madison Books, 2002), and *Women of Color* by Darlene Mathis (SPCK and Triangle, 1999). Susan Fignar recommends *Image Consulting: The New Career* by Joan Timberlake (Acropolis Books, 1983), which discusses the various areas in which image consultants specialize. Because networking is so important in getting clients, she also suggests *Networlding: Building Relationships and Opportunities for Success* by Melissa Giovagnoli (Jossey-Bass, 2000). Local libraries should have additional books on color, fabrics, style, etiquette, and body language.

Employers

For the most part, color analysts and image consultants are self-employed. They run their own consulting businesses, which allows them the freedom to decide what image consulting services they wish to offer. For example, some consultants concentrate on working with corporate clients; other consultants may also advise individuals. Consultants may get the products they sell from one company, such as Color Me Beautiful, or they may offer a range of products and services that provide ways for clients to feel good about themselves. Those in apprenticeships and consultants just entering the field may work for consultants who have already established their businesses.

Starting Out

Some consultants enter the field through apprenticeships. Susan Fignar began by working in advertising, where she had extensive experience in meeting planning and often was responsible for company visitors. She eventually attended a training program on fashion and image consulting. She says there are many routes to entering this field.

Advancement

Workers can advance from color analysts to image consultants to trainers by gaining experience and additional education. Christine Sherlock began as an apprentice and has advanced through various positions with Color Me Beautiful. Salon and department store employees would advance along the path their employers have laid out.

Susan Fignar hopes to expand her business by adding new clients, taking advantage of new trends, developing training for future image consultants, and forming alliances with consultants who offer related services. This is par for the course for all self-employed analysts and consultants. She has had her own business for seven years and says it takes three to five years to get a corporate consulting business established.

Earnings

A color analyst's or image consultant's earnings are determined by the number of hours the consultant works, the type of clientele, and the consultant's location. Christine Sherlock says earnings are highest in New York City and southern California. Some consultants increase their incomes by offering additional services. Susan Fignar estimates that earnings start at under $20,000 but can reach $75,000 or more for top performers. Since many color analysts and image consultants own their own businesses, it may also be helpful to consider that some small business owners may earn only about $15,000 a year, while the most successful may make $100,000 or more.

Sherlock points out such advantages as owning your own business, flexible hours, controlling your own time, and opportunity for personal growth and development. Because most consultants are self-employed, they must provide their own insurance and other benefits.

Work Environment

Many consultants work out of their homes. Color consultants also work in salons, boutiques, day spas, and retail areas. The work is indoors and may involve travel. Christine Sherlock comments that the work has changed her life and that she loves everything she has done in the field.

Susan Fignar works at corporate sites and training facilities, speaks before various organizations, and has appeared on radio and television. She has contact with management and with human resources and training departments. Her work schedule has busy and slow periods, but she usually works from 40 to 50 hours a week and sometimes makes evening presentations. She describes her work as exciting, draining, and full of time constraints.

Outlook

The employment of personal appearance workers is expected to grow at an average rate through 2010, according to the *Occupational Outlook Handbook,* mainly due to increasing population, incomes, and demand for cosmetology services.

Christine Sherlock says the economy has little effect on color consulting. During sluggish times, people still want the lift that such beauty services give them. The demand for consultants is growing steadily, and she believes self-employed people with successful businesses aren't likely to be out of work. The field is evolving, with new opportunities in corporate work.

Susan Fignar says corporate consultants are affected by downsizing because when companies cut personnel they also reduce training. "Right now," she says, "the field is growing." She says the hot topics are casual dress for business, etiquette, communications, and public image. Fignar feels security comes from constantly working to build your consulting business. She advises consultants to develop a 60-second sales pitch so they're always ready to describe their services to any prospective client they meet.

For More Information

This organization has information on continuing education and mentorship programs as well as a listing of programs that offer certificates upon completion.

ASSOCIATION OF IMAGE CONSULTANTS INTERNATIONAL
International Headquarters
2695 Villa Creek Drive, Suite 260
Dallas, TX 75234
Tel: 972-755-1503
Email: info@aici.org
Web: http://www.aici.org

This company provides information on contacting local consultants. Check out its Web site for information on its products.

COLOR ME BEAUTIFUL
14000 Thunderbolt Place, Suite E
Chantilly, VA 20151
Tel: 800-265-6763
Web: http://www.colormebeautiful.com

Cosmetic Surgeons

Overview

Cosmetic surgeons (also known as *plastic surgeons* or *esthetic surgeons*) are medical doctors who specialize in surgeries to correct disfigurement and/or improve physical appearance. Though the terms cosmetic and plastic surgery are often used interchangeably, cosmetic surgery usually means procedures performed to reshape normal structures of the body to improve the patient's appearance. Plastic surgery generally refers to reconstructive surgeries performed on abnormal structures of the body caused by birth defects, developmental abnormalities, trauma, injury, infection, tumors, or disease. There are approximately 4,200 cosmetic surgeons working in the United States.

History

Contrary to popular belief, cosmetic surgery is not a recent development. Although the increase in the popularity of certain cosmetic procedures is a relatively new trend, surgeons have been correcting human disfigurement since 3400 BC, when Egyptian healers performed cosmetic operations on the face, feet, and arms. Another ancient tie can be found in the profession's own name. The "plastic" in plastic surgery does not mean "artificial." Rather, plastic surgery derives its name from the ancient Greek word plastikos, which meant to mold or give form. In fact, the modern-day "nose job," which Hollywood celebrities seem to favor, likely got its start in ancient India, although the procedures done at that time were for reconstructive rather than strictly cosmetic purposes. By 800 BC, physicians in India were using skin grafts (a process that transfers healthy skin from one part of the body to another for the purpose of replacing damaged or lost skin) to perform reconstructive work for facial injuries.

Cosmetic surgery changed little during the Dark Ages but began to develop again in the 1700s, when British surgeons introduced to Europe techniques they had seen in India. Further improvement in skin grafting techniques continued, but progress was slow until the early 1900s.

Before World War I, the profession evolved slowly in North America as well. Virginian Dr. John Peter Mettauer performed the first cleft palate operation in the New World in 1827 with instruments he designed himself. With the advent of world war, physicians were challenged to find ways to treat extensive facial and head injuries never before seen, such as shattered jaws and gaping skull wounds.

It wasn't until the late 1930s that the American Board of Surgeons, the medical certifying organization of the time, established a specialty board to certify cosmetic surgeons—the American Board of Plastic Surgery—with its own standards and specialized training. Prior to the establishment of this board, many physicians who performed reconstructive surgeries were from other specialties related to cosmetic surgery.

New techniques developed in the 1950s included internal wiring for facial fractures and rotation flaps for skin deformities. In the 1960s, the scope of procedures performed by surgeons widened as the public became more informed. Cosmetic procedures became more popular. Silicone was initially used to treat skin imperfections and was first used as a breast implant device in 1962. The safety of silicone breast implants has since come into question, and its use for breast implants was banned in 1992. The 1980s saw plastic surgeons expand their efforts to bring information to the public, and in the 1990s, the profession focused efforts on having reconstructive procedures covered under health plans.

Despite the many advances, the field is still evolving. Today, researchers are trying to unlock the secrets of the growth-factor environment of the womb, where scarless healing takes place, in order to apply the technique to wounds of children and adults.

The Job

Doctors, especially specialists such as cosmetic surgeons, generally work long hours. Surgeries of all types demand strict attention to detail, and cosmetic surgeries in which the emphasis is on the quality of the patient's appearance can be especially challenging. Still, the profession offers high earnings and personal rewards. Physicians tend to be people who thrive on challenge and are willing to devote a lot of time to their careers.

Of course, cosmetic surgeons don't spend all their working hours in surgery. Daily tasks include patient consultation and record keeping, among other duties. Also, no matter what setting a surgeon practices in, he or she is likely to have administrative duties as well. Surgeons in private practice have an office to manage with duties ranging from hiring employees to marketing the practice to overseeing upkeep of the office. Surgeons who work in a hospital's plastic surgery department have commitments to the hospital outside of performing surgeries and seeing patients. For example, cosmetic surgeons frequently are required to provide general hospital emergency room coverage and split up this task with the other surgeons.

Dr. Richard Maloney, a cosmetic surgeon who practices at the Aesthetic Surgery Center in Naples, Florida, estimates he spends about 60 percent of his time in surgery. Other time is spent on patient visits, follow-up, initial consultations, and emergency room coverage. Maloney acknowledge that many in the field of medicine push themselves to work days as long as 16 hours, seven days a week, but he says that doctors can and should decide how much time they want to devote to work and follow that.

"In the field of medicine, the urge to take on a workload to prove yourself is great. I think the average workweek can be as much as you want it to be," Maloney says. In practice for 19 years, Maloney says he has found 10-hour days provide a good balance between his personal and professional life.

Today's cosmetic surgeons perform a wider range of procedures than their counterparts did only a few decades ago. Previously, the profession focused on reconstructive surgeries, with a few surgeons catering to those who could afford cosmetic procedures. Today, cosmetic surgeries are no longer only for celebrities or the wealthy. The public has become familiar with terms such as liposuction (removal of unwanted fatty deposits), implants, and facelift because those procedures have become more accessible to the general population. According to the American Society of Plastic Surgeons (ASPS), the top five cosmetic procedures in 2000 were nose reshaping, liposuction, eyelid surgery, breast augmentation, and facelift. And as cosmetic surgery becomes more commonplace, an increasing number of men are having it done. Nose reshaping, hair transplants, breast reduction, and ear surgery are some of the most popular procedures among men, according to the ASPS. Today's cosmetic surgeons perform more strictly cosmetic procedures than the average cosmetic surgeon did even a decade ago. Of course, a surgeon can still choose to specialize in reconstructive surgery, but trends indicate growth in the field is certainly with all types of cosmetic procedures.

There are different settings in which a cosmetic surgeon may work. Three arrangements are common. The first is private practice, in which the surgeon is the sole physician in a practice with his or her own staff. The physician performs surgeries either in his or her own clinic or at a hospital where he or she has privileges. The second is group practice, in which a surgeon is part of a group of cosmetic surgeons or other related specialists who market their services together. Group practice surgeons may also perform surgeries in their own clinic or at a hospital. The third common arrangement is working in hospital departments, where a surgeon is a member of a hospital's plastic surgery department. A less common career path for a cosmetic surgeon who has considerable surgical experience is a professorship at an academic institution or teaching hospital.

Because plastic surgery is a highly specialized field, plastic surgeons generally work in urban areas, both large and small. Most rural areas don't have enough patients to create a reasonable demand. The ASPS estimates that over half of its 5,000 members work in large metropolitan areas.

Requirements

HIGH SCHOOL

If you want to pursue a career in medicine, prepare yourself by learning the self-discipline to concentrate on schoolwork in high school in order to achieve the grades necessary to gain entrance to a good undergraduate program. Performing well at the college level can help you compete for slots in medical school. Start working hard in high school by taking college preparatory classes such as mathematics, including algebra and geometry, and sciences, including biology, chemistry, and physics. Also, consider taking a foreign language. Many college programs have foreign language requirements, and a familiarity with some foreign languages may help you with your medical studies later on. Finally, don't forget to take English courses. These classes will help you develop your research and writing skills—two skills that will be essential to you in your career.

In addition, check out school clubs and civic organizations that offer volunteer opportunities for students in places such as local hospitals or nursing homes. In addition to the experience you will get by volunteering, you will also have the opportunity to establish valuable relationships with people who work in the health care field. Clubs such as Kiwanis, Rotary, and Lions often count community leaders such as doctors, hospital administrators, and other health care professionals among their members. Many of these clubs have charter clubs in high schools, and student members have regular contact with these community leaders.

POSTSECONDARY TRAINING
Training to become a doctor is a rigorous, lengthy process. After high school, students pursuing a career in medicine can expect to spend eleven to sixteen years in school and training before they can practice medicine. Requirements include four years of undergraduate school, four years of medical school, and three to eight years of residency. Not all students who apply to medical school are accepted, and many go on to other careers in the field of medicine. Entry to medical school is very competitive, and prospective students must show they possess exceptional academic abilities. Medical schools also consider character, personality, leadership qualities, and participation in extracurricular activities when deciding whether to accept a student.

The minimum education requirement for entry to a medical school is three years of college, although most applicants have at least a bachelor's degree and many have advanced degrees. Undergraduate degrees obtained by medical school applicants vary, but many have degrees in mathematics, engineering, or sciences such as biology, or in premed. Premedical students complete courses in physics, biology, mathematics, English, and inorganic and organic chemistry. Some students also volunteer at local hospitals or clinics to gain practical experience. This volunteer experience will weigh in a student's favor on competitive medical school applications. Junior and senior years in undergraduate school for students planning to go on to medical school are very busy years. In addition to keeping up with their studies, junior and senior undergraduates often spend much of their time researching medical school programs, volunteering, or gaining other experience that could be helpful on a medical school application. Students should keep in mind that acceptance to medical school is highly competitive. At a top medical school in the nation, for example, the class of 2000 consisted of 104 men and 67 women selected from 8,639 applicants. The students accepted had an average grade point average of 3.5 on a 4.0 scale. Medical school lasts four years, in addition to the four years a student has already put in at the undergraduate level, so those who want to pursue a medical career should be prepared to commit many years to being a student.

All physicians, whether or not they plan to specialize in a field such as cosmetic surgery, must complete additional training. Specialty training, depending on the field, varies from three to eight years. The certifying board for cosmetic surgeons, the American Board of Cosmetic Surgeons (ABCS), requires four years of residency in cosmetic surgery procedures. Traditionally, medical school graduates spend their first graduate year in a hospital internship. This first year of training following medical school is called the PGY-I, during which graduates work long hours to learn about assuming the responsibility for care of patients in the role of a physician. After the first year, students are generally matched up into an internship program known as a residency program. It is during residency that physicians-in-training are introduced to their chosen specialties. Residents work under physicians who are specialists in their chosen fields at a teaching hospital. Medical school graduates must apply to residency programs by ranking their preferences for different hospitals. Independent agencies, such as the National Residency Matching Program, match the student's preferences with the programs for which they are qualified. Accepted residency programs are accredited by the Accreditation Council for Graduate Medical Education.

CERTIFICATION OR LICENSING

All 50 states require physicians be licensed to practice. Certification by one of the 24 certifying boards recognized by the American Board of Medical Specialties is not a legal requirement. Many physicians choose to become certified in their field because certification enables the public to identify practitioners who have met a standard of training and experience beyond the level required for licensure. As consumers become more informed and health care becomes more market-driven, physicians who are board certified are expected to be more in demand. Many patient advocate groups and patient information sources urge patients to choose physicians who are board certified.

The American Board of Cosmetic Surgery certifies physicians in the following areas: I) facial cosmetic surgery, 2) dermatological cosmetic surgery, 3) body and extremity cosmetic surgery, and 4) general cosmetic surgery. Requirements vary slightly for each area, but basic requirements include certification by one of the boards recognized by the American Board of Medical Specialties, a one- or two-year fellowship in an approved program, proof of hospital operating room privileges, and proof of a valid medical license.

OTHER REQUIREMENTS

The field of medicine demands highly disciplined individuals who can perform complex tasks with a high degree of accuracy. Cosmetic surgery requires skill and artistry as well as these talents, according to Dr. Richard Maloney.

"It takes a fastidious person, but not to a fault. There are a lot of steps to the surgical procedures a plastic surgeon performs. Each must be properly executed; if it's not, it amplifies the error in the next step, and so on," Maloney says. "Plastic surgeons do well if they enjoy growing and generating results," he adds. Hard work, self-confidence and dedication are also vital. "It's a very rewarding line of work, but probably the biggest drawback is all of the work and years of schooling it takes to get to this point. But if students are really interested, they should follow their interests and take each hurdle as it comes."

Medicine also requires its successful professionals to have so-called people skills in addition to knowledge and discipline. People are the "objects of the trade" for physicians, and communication skills and the ability to empathize with a wide variety of people are essential. The ability to work as part of a team is also important. A cosmetic surgeon performs surgeries and therefore depends on a surgical team to assist in surgery. The cosmetic surgeon must be able to communicate and work well with colleagues as well as patients.

Exploring

At the high school and undergraduate levels, you can begin to learn about the field of medicine by volunteering at hospitals, nursing homes, or clinics. By working in these settings you will not only have the opportunity to gauge how much you enjoy this type of work, but you will also have the chance to be around professionals in the field.

Another way you can explore is by talking to medical professionals, perhaps by interviewing one for a term paper or other school project. Or you may simply tell a doctor you know that you are interested in his or her profession and request an informational interview. Come to the interview prepared to ask questions. Ask the doctor how he or she got started in the field. What does he or she like most and least about the job? What were the years of school like? People are often happy to talk about their jobs if you show a sincere interest, and you may even discover a mentor in this way.

One national organization, the National Youth Leadership Forum (NYLF), offers an annual forum for high school students interested in a career in medicine. This eleven-day forum, offered several times during the summer, gives students an opportunity to gain hands-on experience in medicine by visiting medical schools, research facilities, and hospitals and talking to people in various stages of the medical career path, from first-year medical students to practicing physicians. NYLF reports the curriculum in its medical forum covers a broad range of topics in medicine, including educational requirements, career options, clinical practice, and current issues facing the profession. Forums are open to juniors and seniors with 3.3 or above grade point averages. Teachers and guidance counselors recommend 95 percent of students accepted for forums. Students may ask about the program at their school or contact the organization themselves. Tuition fees and travel expenses apply, as NYLF is a nonprofit organization, but many students are able to find sponsors in their community.

Employers

When a cosmetic surgeon works in private practice, either alone or with a group of other specialists offering their services, the surgeon is essentially self-employed and running his or her own business. Surgeons may also work for hospitals, health maintenance organizations (HMOs), or the government, such as at the Department of Veterans Affairs. In addition, universities employ a number of surgeons in academic positions.

Starting Out

There is really only one way to enter the field of medicine. All physicians are required to have a medical degree. Beyond that, one's options for entering various specialties increase. Four years of residency training is required of all surgeons certified by the American Board of Cosmetic Surgery (ABCS). However, the nature of that residency training, and to some extent, the location, may be up to the individual.

Many cosmetic surgeons participate in residency programs and take the exam to become board certified in cosmetic surgery. The ABCS offers certification opportunities to specialists in other fields, including general surgery, gynecology, otolaryngology, oral and maxillofacial surgery, dermatology, and ophthalmology. These specialties are related to many specific plastic surgery procedures and provide a different avenue of entering the field. Physicians certified in these fields are generally limited to performing surgeries in their specialty areas (for example, dermatologists would perform burn repair surgery or other graft surgery, but they are not likely to perform liposuction).

Advancement

Once physicians become licensed as cosmetic surgeons, their opportunities for advancement are largely up to them. For many cosmetic surgeons, if they have not already done so, becoming board certified by the American Board of Cosmetic Surgeons is a first step in advancing their careers. As consumers become more informed about their options for cosmetic surgery, cosmetic surgeons with added credentials such as board certifications are likely to be in higher demand. Many associations, such as the American Society of Plastic Surgeons (ASPS), offer a screening service for consumers, who can check a cosmetic surgeon's qualifications when choosing a surgeon.

Any further training a cosmetic surgeon undergoes, such as the additional years of residency required to learn a subspecialty, will increase his or her earnings.

Cosmetic surgeons who are part of a hospital's cosmetic surgery department may have opportunities for advancement within their department or to a higher position at other hospitals. Generally, cosmetic surgeons who are promoted within their departments have years of experience. Some do research outside of their surgery duties and publish their works in medical journals. Others teach cosmetic surgery at universities or become part of the staff to teach residents in a teaching hospital.

Some cosmetic surgeons with years of experience go on to chair cosmetic surgery departments at major hospitals or universities, spending less time on cosmetic surgery and more time on administrative duties and research.

Earnings

It takes many years of training to become a doctor, but earnings are among the highest of any occupation. For doctors, more so than for other fields, the number of years of training directly correlates with the earnings level. Specialists, such as cosmetic surgeons, generally earn more money than general practitioners. The more specialized the field, the higher the earnings.

For the most part, general surgeons have earnings ranging from $150,000 to $250,000. The latest data available from the American Medical Association notes that surgeons (of all types) had a median income of $240,000 in 1998. *Medical Economics,* a magazine for medical professionals, featured a September 17, 2001, article on earnings of doctors in office-based private practice. The earnings survey conducted by the magazine reveals that general surgeons had a median annual gross income of $370,640 in 2000. After expenses, their median income was $199,690. Cosmetic surgeons, who are specialists, can be expected to have earnings somewhat higher than those of general surgeons. In addition, experience also translates into higher income levels. According to the recruitment firm Physicians Search (http://www.physicianssearch.com), responses for its *Physician Compensation Survey—In Practice Three Plus Years* show that plastic surgeons with three-plus years' experience averaged $306,047 annually in 2001. The lowest paid respondent specializing in plastic surgery earned $196,711 per year, and the highest paid had an annual income of $411,500, also in 2001.

Cosmetic surgeons, and physicians in general, enjoy generous health care benefits. Other benefits may include recruitment bonuses, pay for continuing education, and forgiveness of school loans. Although they work long hours throughout the year, physicians are often granted several weeks' paid vacation and other leave time as relief from the demanding jobs they have.

Work Environment

There are advantages to working in the different work arrangements available to a plastic surgeon (private practice, group practice, hospital department, or government or academic setting). A surgeon's preference may depend on how he or she works with others, as well as geographic location. Hospital plastic surgery departments are usually structured with department chairs and supervisors. Although a hospital setting generally means more rules for a physician to work under, it also offers the advantage of a structured environment, less individual financial risk, and the ability to share information and learn from colleagues daily. Those who prefer to be "their own boss" generally assume greater risk in a private or group practice, as does any small business owner. Plastic surgeons in private or group practice should be business oriented or hire someone who can tend to marketing, accounting, and personnel concerns.

As with many specialists, cosmetic surgeons generally practice in big cities or smaller urban areas, but not in rural areas. Big-city settings generally bring advantages such as proximity to colleagues and shorter traveling distance to seminars and the hours of continuing education required of board-certified surgeons every year. Urban life brings increased cultural and recreational opportunities, but it can also mean headaches such as traffic and a higher cost of living.

Cosmetic surgeons, compared with other specialists, are not in frequent contact with contagious disease or hazardous chemicals. Some cosmetic procedures require the use of chemicals for injections or surface application, but surgeons are well trained and well regulated in their use of these materials.

The profession is not without its opportunities for service to humanity, but it is often these situations that put a cosmetic surgeon in contact with some dangers. Areas where people suffer from contagious disease and political violence in remote parts of developing countries are often the areas of greatest need for reconstructive surgeries. A program affiliated with the ASPS, the Reconstructive Surgeons Volunteer Program, sends U.S. surgeons to such areas. Surgeons perform vital work there on people who have no hope of getting help from their own country, but the surgeons' accommodations often include only the bare essentials. Extreme weather, insects, and the sound of shots being fired in the distance are situations some surgeons have encountered.

Outlook

According to the U.S. Department of Labor, the demand for all physicians is expected to grow about as fast as the average through 2010. Because of population trends that include a rapidly aging population, physicians who meet the needs of older Americans can expect to see a steady demand for their services. Cosmetic surgeons, who treat conditions associated with aging and help older people maintain a youthful appearance, can be counted among medical specialists who will be in strong demand by the aging baby boomer population.

According to statistics compiled by the ASPS, the market for these surgeons is large: in 2000 alone, 7.4 million people had cosmetic plastic surgery, and more than 6 million had reconstructive surgery. Men make up a growing clientele, accounting for 14 percent of the cosmetic surgery performed in 2000.

For More Information

To learn about cosmetic procedures and recent statistics, contact:
AMERICAN ACADEMY OF COSMETIC SURGERY
737 North Michigan Avenue, Suite 820
Chicago, IL 60611
Tel: 312-981-6760
Web: http://www.cosmeticsurgery.org

Among this foundation's goals are promoting high standards of training, conferring scholarships, and increasing public education in plastic surgery matters.
AMERICAN SOCIETY OF PLASTIC SURGEONS AND THE PLASTIC SURGERY EDUCATIONAL FOUNDATION
444 East Algonquin Road
Arlington Heights, IL 60005
Tel: 847-228-9900
Web: http://www.plasticsurgery.org

This association is devoted to providing information about medical schools in the United States.

ASSOCIATION OF AMERICAN MEDICAL COLLEGES
2450 N Street, NW
Washington, DC 20037-1126
Tel: 202-828-0400
Web: http://www.aamc.org

This organization offers career programs to high school students interested in the medical profession. Forums are offered in Atlanta, Chicago, Boston, Houston-Galveston, Philadelphia, Los Angeles, and Washington, DC. Visit the Web site for information on schedule dates.

NATIONAL YOUTH LEADERSHIP FORUM
2020 Pennsylvania Avenue, NW
Washington, DC 20006
Tel: 202-347-4036
Email: nylf@nylf.org
Web: http://www.nylf.org

Cosmeticians

School Subjects
  Biology
  Chemistry
Personal Skills
  Artistic
  Following instructions
Work Environment
  Primarily indoors
  Primarily one location
Minimum Education Level
  Some postsecondary training
Salary Range
  $13,000 to $20,080 to $50,000
Certification or Licensing
  Required by certain states
Outlook
  About as fast as the average

Overview

Cosmeticians specialize in skin care, providing facial masks, peels, herbal wraps, massages, skin analysis, exfoliation, product recommendations, and makeup application. In addition, cosmeticians provide hair removal services. Most cosmeticians work in beauty salons, day spas, and hotel resorts. Some work with dermatologists and cosmetic surgeons to prepare patients before surgery and during their recovery. There are approximately 21,000 cosmeticians working in the United States.

History

The role of the cosmetician today originates from a long history of pampering and leisurely self-care, which began centuries ago in the public baths and spas of Asia and Europe. Ancient Babylonians, Egyptians, and Romans renewed and invigorated themselves in public baths. Archeological evidence suggests that in ancient Egypt cosmetics were also used to enhance the appearance of the skin. Products included ingredients such as special soils, wax, honey, and oils that were formulated into masks, makeup, and lipsticks. In ancient Greece, Hippocrates, known as the father of medicine, contributed to the development of *esthetics* (scientific skin care). Archeological remains suggest that Greek women used mixtures of plant roots and yeast to try to eliminate freckles and applied masks made with bread crumbs and milk to prevent wrinkles. Artifacts from ancient Roman society include recipes for creams made from fruit juices, honey, and olive oil. Soothing therapies, still practiced today, from shiatsu massages to potent herbal treatments, have been passed down from thousand-year-old traditions of the East.

During the Middle Ages interest in skin care and public baths waned in the Western world. Certain orders of nuns, however, devoted themselves to producing beauty products to support their convents. Perfume oils began to be used, and the fragrance market was launched. The Renaissance saw skin care and cosmetics again become popular in large European cities. The manufacture of perfumes became a major industry. From writings of the 16th century, we find that many formulas and mixtures are very similar to modern cosmetic products. By the 17th and 18th centuries spas had gained the support of the medical establishment and once again became popular places. And by the 1800s, Europe's wealthy classes were spending months at a time relaxing and rejuvenating themselves at spas. It was not until the 1920s that spas caught on in the United States, and even then visiting a spa was a luxury only the very wealthy could afford.

Today, due to heightened health awareness, the need for more specialized beauty services, and the increasing affordability of spa and salon services in the United States, cosmeticians are more in demand than ever before. Now more than just pamperers, cosmeticians are professionals and consultants, equipped with an awareness of skin conditions and allergies as well as the scientific knowledge necessary to make recommendations based on biological and chemical analysis. As technical advancements in such areas as chemical peels and wrinkle reduction continue to boom, cosmeticians will become more prevalent, and their services will be in greater demand.

The Job

Cosmeticians may also be known as *estheticians* (also spelled *aestheticians*) or *skin care specialists*. The word *esthetic* comes from the Greek word meaning harmony, beauty, and perfection. Esthetics is based on an understanding of the skin's anatomy and function. Cosmeticians work to improve the skin's condition and restore its functions. This discipline requires the cosmetician to get to know the client's skin and lifestyle and to tailor treatments specifically for the client's needs. Cosmeticians offer a number of appearance-enhancing services that deal with the effects pollution, lack of exercise, poor nutrition, and stress have on the skin. The cosmetician's job may involve facials, massages, wraps and packs, hydrotherapy treatments, scalp treatments, hair removal services, color analysis, makeup services, and product sales. Before beginning to work with a client, the cosmetician will most likely consult with the individual to determine his or her goals and concerns. It is important that cosmeticians are clear with their clients as to what they should expect from their treatments.

Before beginning treatment, the cosmetician must determine the client's needs. After the initial consultation for a facial, for instance, the cosmetician will need to perform a skin analysis in order to assess the client's water and oil levels and skin conditions—whether there are blackheads, lines, wrinkles, etc. Once this information is determined, pre-cleansing, deep cleansing, exfoliation (the removal of dead skin), and extractions may follow, depending on the client's skin type. Cosmeticians often blend special cleansers and moisturizers themselves, according their clients' individual skin types.

The application of a mask, appropriate for the patron's skin type, may follow the cleansing and exfoliation process, along with neck, facial, and shoulder massages. Foot and hand massages may be included as well. In most states, cosmeticians are licensed to perform only hand, foot, and facial massages, and training for these services is usually provided in cosmetology programs. Full-body massages require both further training and a special license.

While performing such procedures as extractions, which involve the removal of blackheads, whiteheads, and other skin debris, cosmeticians must be careful to protect themselves by using gloves and the proper sanitation. These procedures are covered in cosmetician training programs and are regulated by law in most states.

Other services cosmeticians offer include wraps, packs, and hydrotherapy treatments. Often made of herbs, mud, or algae, these treatments remove or redistribute fat cells and retained body water in order to create a temporarily slimmer look. Some wraps and packs actually remove impurities from the body. Hydrotherapy treatments cleanse the body using sea water, fresh water, hot tubs, whirlpool baths, and hydrotherapy tubs.

Cosmeticians also provide cosmetics and makeup consultation and application services. They may assist clients in deciding what colors and makeup to use and how they should apply it to achieve the best results, whether it's for accentuating their features or covering blemishes.

Hair removal services, usually waxing and tweezing, are also offered. Electrolysis is another popular form of hair removal; however, since a special license is required to perform electrolysis, cosmeticians generally wax and tweeze unwanted hair from the face, eyebrows, and other parts of the body.

In addition to working with clients, cosmeticians are expected to keep their work areas clean and implements sanitized. In smaller salons, many make appointments and assist with day-to-day business activities. In larger salons, cosmeticians must be aware of keeping to appointment schedules. They may have to juggle two or more clients, at different stages of treatment, at the same time.

Salon managers or *salon owners* have managerial responsibilities—accounting and record keeping, hiring, firing, and motivating workers, advertising and public relations, and ordering and stocking supplies and products.

People skills are very important for a cosmetician to have. A critical part of cosmeticians' jobs is to cultivate and maintain a growing clientele for themselves and their salons or spas. Cosmeticians should be sensitive to the client's comfort and have dexterity and a sense of artistry. If the cosmetician's style of skin care is not suited to the client, he or she should be willing to refer the client to another specialist. This builds goodwill toward the cosmetician and the salon or spa.

Requirements

HIGH SCHOOL

If working as a cosmetician interests you, there are a number of classes you can take in high school to prepare for this job. Some vocational high schools offer classes that will prepare you specifically for cosmetology careers. If you are not attending a vocational high school, you should take science classes, such as biology, chemistry, and human anatomy. These classes will give you an understanding of how the body works as well as how chemicals react with each other. Scientific knowledge will come in handy when you consult with your clients about their allergies and skin conditions. In addition, science classes will give you the background necessary for understanding bacteriology and equipment sanitization—subjects you will most likely study in cosmetician courses following high school. Since you will be working with many different clients in this career, consider taking psychology courses, which will give you an understanding of people and their motivations. Take English and speech classes to develop your communication skills. Finally, take art courses. Art courses will allow you to work with your hands and help you develop your sense of color.

POSTSECONDARY TRAINING

Once you have completed high school, plan on enrolling in an accredited cosmetology school. A school's accreditation by the National Accrediting Commission of Cosmetology Arts and Sciences means that the school is meeting educational standards set by this national organization. It is important to make sure you will be going to a good school because having a solid education from a respected program is one of your strongest assets when entering this field. You should also be aware of the licensing requirements for the state in which you hope to work. Make sure that the school you are interested in will allow you to meet these requirements. Depending on the school you choose to attend, you may enter a full cosmetology program to later specialize as a cosmetician, or you may enroll in a cosmetician or esthetician program. In either case, your education should include study in skin care, massage techniques, specific areas of the law pertaining to the field, sanitation methods, makeup, and salon management.

CERTIFICATION OR LICENSING

A cosmetician needs a license in most states, though the process, laws, and requirements vary from state to state. Licensing usually involves a test of one's skill and knowledge. A few states have reciprocity agreements, which would allow licensed cosmeticians to practice in a different state without additional formal training.

OTHER REQUIREMENTS

A friendly, people-oriented personality and good listening skills are essential for this business. Because cosmeticians must work very closely with their clients, interpersonal skills are important. Sensitivity, tactfulness, and patience are particularly vital, especially when dealing with clients who may be unhappy about their appearance or clients who have unreasonable expectations.

Flexibility is also a necessary trait, considering the long and irregular hours a full-time cosmetician works. Furthermore, the ability to sell has also become a desirable characteristic in cosmeticians because retail sales are becoming a large part of salon offerings. Finally, a cosmetician should enjoy learning, as he or she may need to take continuing educa-

tion workshops or seminars in order to keep up with licensing requirements and new developments in the field.

Exploring

One of the first activities you may consider in exploring this career is to
get a facial or other service provided by a cosmetician. As a client yourself, you will be able to observe the work setting and actually experience
the procedure. Often people are best at providing services when they
enjoy receiving the service or believe in its benefits.

Next, you may want to research this field by looking at association
and trade magazines—the publications cosmeticians read to stay current with their field's trends. Trade publications will give you an idea of
what current technical, legal, and fashion issues cosmeticians face.

You may choose to contact cosmetology schools to find out about
cosmetician or esthetician programs in your area. Request informational brochures or course listings from the schools and speak to school
advisors about the training involved and the nature of the work. A good
way to locate cosmetology schools is to conduct an Internet search.

Also, once you have found a cosmetology school you are interested in, ask to set up an informational interview with an instructor or
recent graduate. Go to the interview prepared to ask questions. What is
the training like? What does this person enjoy about the job? What is the
most difficult aspect of the work? By asking such questions you may be
able to determine if the field is right for you.

You may also be able to set up an informational interview with a
cosmetician who works at a spa or salon near you. Again, go to the
interview prepared with questions. By networking in this fashion, you
may also develop a mentor relationship. Then you may be able to spend
time with your mentor at his or her place of work and observe everyday
activities.

Getting a part-time position at a salon or spa on weekends or after
school is an excellent way of exploring the field. Because you are working at the spa or salon on a regular basis, you will learn more about what
various jobs are like and how the business functions. While on the job,
you can observe the interaction between clients and cosmeticians, the
interaction among co-workers, the different levels of management, and
the general atmosphere. This can help you decide whether this is an area
you would like to explore further.

Employers

Approximately 21,000 cosmeticians are employed in the United States, and they work in a variety of business settings that provide beauty, fitness and health, or personal care services. They may work for salons, fitness centers, and spas, as well as at resorts, at large hotels, and even on cruise ships. Some work for cosmetology schools as instructors of esthetics. Those with experience and interest in having their own business may decide to run their own salon where they offer a variety of services.

Starting Out

After completing a cosmetician or cosmetology program and passing state board exams, you can seek a position as an entry-level cosmetician. Cosmeticians find their jobs through cosmetology schools—salons and spas often recruit directly from schools. Networking in the field is also a viable option for aspiring cosmeticians looking for good work. Reading trade publication classified ads is also a way to locate job openings. Salons and spas most often advertise open positions in newspaper classifieds. There are also some placement agencies that match cosmetologists with salons and spas looking for workers.

Advancement

Upon first entering the field, a cosmetician will advance somewhat as he or she gains clientele. A large and steady clientele will translate into higher earnings and greater professional status.

Beyond the entry-level cosmetician, one can move up to director of cosmeticians (often called director of estheticians). Eventually a cosmetician or esthetician can become a spa or salon manager, then move up to spa or salon director. For many cosmeticians, an ultimate goal is to own a spa or salon. Some cosmeticians open their own salons after being certified and without having to work up the ranks of another spa or salon.

As an alternative to working in a salon or spa, some cosmeticians decide to teach in cosmetology schools or use their knowledge to demonstrate cosmetics and skin care products in department stores. Others become cosmetics sales representatives or start businesses as beauty consultants. Some cosmeticians work as examiners for state cosmetology boards.

Earnings

The U.S. Department of Labor, which groups cosmeticians with barbers, cosmetologists, and workers specializing in personal appearance services, reports that cosmeticians working full-time had an annual median income of $20,080 (including tips) in 2000. However, salaries for cosmeticians vary widely based on where they work, the method of payment (commission and tips only or commission, salary, and tips), and the clientele. Those working on commission and tips only will find their beginning incomes very low as they work to build a steady clientele. In addition, not every company provides health benefits, which adds extra costs for the entry-level cosmetician who may already be struggling. Some companies pay a salary plus commission, which obviously is better for the entry-level cosmetician who has yet to establish a clientele. Some salaries start at or near minimum wage. When tips are added in, cosmeticians may end up with yearly incomes somewhere between $13,000 and $15,000. Other base salaries may reach the lower to mid-$20,000s.

It is usually not until the cosmetician reaches a manager's or director's position that he or she will make upwards of $50,000.

Work Environment

Despite the fact that the field seems elite and glamorous, being a cosmetician is hard work. Through most of the day cosmeticians must work on their feet. Some days are relaxing, while others are quite hectic. Cosmeticians and salon owners can easily work more than 40 hours per week. Weekend and lunch-hour time slots are often especially busy. According to Liza Wong, owner of Elite Skin Care, a salon in San Mateo, California, time management is the most difficult aspect of the job. "Cosmeticians must be flexible and willing to work late evenings and on weekends, around their clients' work schedules," says Wong.

On the positive side, it is a very social position. Cosmeticians see a variety of clients each day and perform a variety of services. They learn a lot from their clients—about their lives and their jobs.

Outlook

Liza Wong predicts a big future for cosmeticians. "Americans are just starting to become aware of this field," Wong says. "These services, once only enjoyed by the rich, are becoming more affordable, and as baby boomers are trying to keep their youth and maintain their skin, there will be an increasing demand for skin care." The U.S. Department of Labor predicts employment growth for cosmeticians to be about as fast as the average through 2010. The growing popularity and affordability of day spas that offer full services should provide job opportunities for skin care specialists.

Spending for personal care services is considered by most people to be discretionary. Therefore, during hard economic times, people tend to visit cosmeticians less frequently, which reduces earnings. However, rarely are good cosmeticians laid off solely because of economic downturns.

For More Information

For information on publications and continuing education, contact:
AESTHETICS' INTERNATIONAL ASSOCIATION
PO Box 468
Kaufman, TX 75142
Tel: 877-968-7539
Email: AIAthekey@aol.com
Web: http://www.beautyworks.com/aia

For industry news, a listing of accredited schools, and information on financial aid, contact:
NATIONAL ACCREDITING COMMISSION OF COSMETOLOGY
ARTS AND SCIENCES
4401 Ford Avenue, Suite 1300
Alexandria, VA 22302-1432
Tel: 703-600-7600
Web: http://www.naccas.org

For more industry news, contact:
NATIONAL COSMETOLOGY ASSOCIATION
401 North Michigan Avenue, 22nd Floor
Chicago, IL 60611
Tel: 312-527-6765
Web: http://www.salonprofessionals.org

For a listing of schools by state, check out the following Web site:
BEAUTYSCHOOL.COM
Web: http://www.beautyschools.com

For hair styling tips and techniques, job listings, and business advice, visit the following Web site:
BEHIND THE CHAIR
Web: http://www.behindthechair.com

Cosmetics Sales Representatives

Quick Facts

School Subjects
Business
Speech

Personal Skills
Artistic
Helping/teaching

Work Environment
Primarily indoors
One location with some travel

Minimum Education Level
Some postsecondary training

Salary Range
$16,680 to $30,000 to $150,000

Certification or Licensing
None available

Outlook
About as fast as the average

Overview

Cosmetics sales representatives demonstrate and sell beauty-care products. Representatives may work from their homes as independent contractors, or they may work in retail establishments where they are employees of the store as well as employees of a cosmetics company.

History

As long ago as 3000 BC, Egyptian priests prepared cosmetics for their kings. Their toiletries and other luxuries were entombed with them. When the tombs of these long-dead kings were excavated in modern times, vases of scented ointments were found, some still holding their fragrant contents. From the kings the use of cosmetics spread. Egyptian women painted their eyebrows, eyelids, and lashes black with kohl. The cosmetics were made of such naturally occurring substances as sesame oil, olive oil, and floral and herbal scents, ingredients that were available to use in simple preparations. Henna was used to color the body or hair red, and white lead or chalk were used to whiten the complexion. From the Middle East and the Mediterranean, the use of cosmetics spread through the Greeks to the Roman Empire and throughout Europe. The change from simple preparations of natural ingredients to the modern industry began in France toward the end of the 19th century. The development of new techniques in manufacturing, packaging, advertising, and marketing has spread cosmetics—and their representatives—around the world.

The Job

Cosmetics sales representatives, or *beauty advisers*, help customers choose particular products appropriate to them. Cosmetics sales reps may consider the condition of the hair, the skin, and the coloring to recommend the cosmetics that will achieve the results desired by the customer. They also introduce the client to new products or techniques. These reps are usually women, but men are also welcome to pursue this career.

Beauty advisers who work in department or specialty stores usually work full-time. They are hired by the store and the cosmetics company, and both provide ongoing training and education. They display, restock, and sell products, attend meetings to learn about new campaigns for different seasons and holidays, attend training sessions, and meet the attendance and performance goals set by the store and by the cosmetics company.

Cosmetics sales representatives who work for such companies as Avon or Mary Kay are not employees but independent contractors who usually work part-time. The goal remains to sell the products, and this job is appealing to those who want to supplement their incomes while keeping their hours flexible. Avon representatives usually distribute fliers or brochures within a specified territory. They take orders by phone or in person. The orders are delivered to the rep, who then delivers them to the customer and collects the money. Mary Kay, another home-based business, also uses flyers to advertise products, and it offers additional services such as skin care classes and facials.

Requirements

HIGH SCHOOL

There are a number of classes you can take in high school to help prepare you for a sales career. Naturally, business classes can be beneficial. A knowledge of business practices and procedures will help you understand the industry. Speech and English classes as well as experience on a debating club will help you develop better communication skills. Also, you should consider taking psychology classes because selling requires an insightful knowledge of people and an ability to read the customer. Computer courses are useful, since retail stores now use computerized record-keeping, and a course in accounting can help independent cosmetics sales representatives better manage their businesses.

POSTSECONDARY TRAINING
Most of the beauty advisers who work for cosmetics companies in retail stores have college degrees or are working toward them. Business or marketing are possible majors for those in this field. Typically, some on-the-job training is involved for new employees at retail stores. There are no specific educational requirements for independent contractors, although some organizations, such as Mary Kay, offer materials and support to help their contractors learn about new products and improve their selling techniques. There is an age requirement of 18 for virtually all cosmetics sales representatives.

OTHER REQUIREMENTS
An outgoing, enthusiastic person who enjoys talking with a variety of new people will enjoy this work. Good manners and being a team player are important. Someone with color blindness, asthma, or allergies—especially to perfumes—should probably not consider this line of work. And, of course, you need a strong back to lift all those boxes of cosmetics.

Exploring

There are entry-level jobs available nationwide. Talking to a cosmetics representative is as easy as picking up the telephone. Both Avon and Mary Kay encourage and reward recruitment of other reps. Mary Kay requires the building of a team or unit of reps. Avon offers job applications on its home page on the Internet.

For jobs in stores, hiring is done by both the store and the cosmetics line, so it is possible to be hired by the cosmetics firm and placed in a store or to be hired by the store and recommended to the cosmetics firm. Personnel offices of stores can be reached by phone or in person for information and employment applications. Current representatives of those companies that are hiring are usually happy to talk to people who might be interested in joining their team or unit.

Employers

Cosmetics sales representatives are usually either self-employed, employed by department stores, or employed by cosmetics companies. It is easy to begin work as an independent contractor for companies such as Avon or Mary Kay. It may be difficult to do this exclusively, however, without supplemental income. Jobs with department stores offer better income security and benefits, but these are usually full-time positions requiring evenings and weekends. Since cosmetics sales continue to increase, as do retail sales in general, there will probably be an abundance of opportunities for those seeking regular employment with stores or cosmetics companies and for independent representatives alike. Unlike most jobs in the cosmetology industry, however, independent cosmetics sales representatives in remote or rural areas may do well due to a lack of department stores and retail establishments specializing in cosmetics.

Starting Out

Patrick Cummings became an Avon representative several years ago. He paid a one-time fee of $20 to begin. "My idea was to make a couple of extra bucks." Pat owns a specialty meat market, and orders and deliveries come to him at the store; he believes that "people don't want or expect other people to come to their homes anymore." Now his customers can pick up their lamb chops and their lipsticks at the same location.

To become a Mary Kay representative, it costs about $100 to buy the sample case. Many of the representatives find most of their customers at their full-time jobs and use cosmetics sales as a supplement to their incomes.

Many cosmetics sales representatives in retail stores start out as perfume spritzers hired by a cosmetics line, or they may be hired during a busy season by the store and then recommended to the cosmetics company.

Advancement

Marianne Blokell began her career in cosmetics over 12 years ago. "I started as a freelance spritzer for Aramis perfume and was hired by Carson, Pirie, Scott, and Co. full time. I worked as a beauty adviser for

Lancome at Carson's, was promoted to counter manager there, and now supervise Lancome counters for two stores." Two avenues of advancement are open to her. She can move up through Lancome from counter manager to account coordinator or account manager in charge of several stores, then to trainer/educator in charge of coaching, training, setting goals, or to account executive. Through Carson's, she can advance to a job as a buyer or a planner.

Earnings

The U.S. Department of Labor reports the median hourly wage, including commission, was $8.02 for all retail sales workers in 2000. A sales rep working full-time at this pay rate would earn approximately $16,680 per year. For cosmetics sales representatives working in stores, earnings vary because each retailer pays differently. Karen Broderick, an account manager for Lancome, offer some average figures. A beginning beauty adviser at Carson, Pirie, Scott, and Co. starts at $6.50 an hour plus 3 percent commission. After five years with a 5 percent raise annually, the average salary is $30,000 to $35,000 a year, which includes in-store incentives, commissions, and bonuses. As the representative rises from counter manager to account manager to account executive for a region, the compensation rises as high as $150,000.

For independent sales representatives, the earnings depend completely on commissions. If they sell nothing, they make nothing. Many independents make only about $100 a month, which is reasonable if they view the job as a supplement, not as their main income.

Work Environment

Cosmetics representatives in retail stores usually work in attractive, climate-controlled settings. But the hours are long, and workers must be on their feet. There is a lot of bending, and there are heavy boxes of stock to unload and display. Cosmetics representatives may not leave the sales floor except at specified times. Many stores have evening and Sunday hours, and breaks and lunch may go by the board in a crush of customers.

Independent contractors usually place orders and accept deliveries at home. They then deliver to their customers, who may be neighbors or co-workers at their primary place of employment.

Outlook

The U.S. Department of Labor predicts job growth for all retail sales reps to be about as fast as the average through 2010. The job picture for cosmetics sales representatives, however, is somewhat mixed. While it is easy to get started in the field, most who choose it work only part-time. Avon alone has about three million representatives selling products in 140 countries. This is a good choice for people needing supplemental income or people in transition, or young mothers who want to stay at home with their children, but most people need an additional job—their own or their spouse's—to provide enough income, health benefits, vacations, or just a day off. Growth in cosmetics companies seems to be international, directed toward opening up new markets in more and more countries; Avon, for example, has stores around the world, from Canada to Thailand, from Greece to Argentina, from Russia to Japan. However, Avon is now also selling cosmetics online, and it remains to be seen how this will affect the company's need for individual sales reps.

Retail selling is such a huge industry that there are always openings to replace those leaving the field, but the hours are long, and the wages start out very low.

For More Information

For information on careers in cosmetics sales, contact or visit the following Web sites:
AVON COSMETICS
Tel: 800-FOR-AVON
Web: http://www.avon.com

MARY KAY COSMETICS
Tel: 800-MARY-KAY
Web: http://www.marykay.com

Cosmetologists

Quick Facts

School Subjects
Art
Business
Speech
Personal Skills
Artistic
Mechanical/manipulative
Work Environment
Primarily indoors
Primarily one location
Minimum Education Level
Some postsecondary training
Salary Range
$12,280 to $17,660 to $33,220+
Certification or Licensing
Required
Outlook
About as fast as the average

Overview

Cosmetologists practice hair-care skills (including washing, cutting, coloring, perming, and applying various conditioning treatments), esthetics (performing skin care treatments), and nail care (grooming of hands and feet). *Barbers* are not cosmetologists but undergo separate training and licensing procedures. According to the U.S. Department of Labor, there are approximately 790,000 cosmetologists, barbers, and other personal appearance services workers employed in the United States.

History

The history of the profession of cosmetology begins with barbering (the Latin *barba* means "beard"), one of the oldest trades, described by writers in ancient Greece. Relics of rudimentary razors date to the Bronze Age, and drawings of people in early Chinese and Egyptian cultures show men with shaved heads, indicating the existence of a barbering profession.

Barbers often did more than hair care. The treatment of illnesses by bloodletting, a task originally performed by monks, was passed along to barbers in 1163 by the papacy. Although trained physicians were already established at this time, they supported and encouraged the use of barbers for routine medical tasks, such as the treatment of wounds and abscesses. From the 12th century to the 18th century, barbers were known as barber-surgeons. They performed medical and surgical services, such as extracting teeth, treating disease, and cauterizing wounds.

Barbers began to organize and form guilds in the 14th century. A barbers' guild was formed in France in 1361. In 1383, the barber of the king of France was decreed to be the head of that guild. The Barbers of London was established as a trade guild in 1462. Barbers distinguished themselves from surgeons and physicians by their titles. Barbers, who were trained through apprenticeships, were referred to as doctors of the short robe; university-trained doctors were doctors of the long robe. In England, during the first part of the 16th century, laws were established to limit the medical activities of barbers. They were allowed to let blood and perform tooth extractions only, while surgeons were banned from performing activities relegated to barbers, such as shaving.

Surgeons separated from the barbers' guild in England and in 1800 established their own guild, the Royal College of Surgeons. Laws were passed to restrict the activities of barbers to nonmedical practices. Barbers continued to be trained through apprenticeships until the establishment of barber training schools at the beginning of the 20th century.

Women did not begin to patronize barbershops until the 1920s. The *bob*, a hairstyle in which women cut their hair just below the ears, became popular at that time. Until that time, women usually wore their hair long. In the 1920s, shorter styles for women became acceptable, and women began to go to barbers for cutting and styling. This opened the door for women to join the profession, and many began training to work with women's hairstyles.

Today, women and a growing number of men patronize hair salons or beauty shops to have their hair cut, styled, and colored. The barbershop, on the other hand, remains largely the domain of men, operated by and for men.

Until the 1920s, *beauticians* (as they were commonly known) performed their services in their clients' homes. The beauty salons and shops now so prevalent have emerged as public establishments in more recent years. In the United States—as in many other countries—the cosmetology business is among the largest of the personal service industries.

The Job

Cosmetology uses hair as a medium to sculpt, perm, color, or design to create a fashion attitude. Hairstylists perform all of these tasks as well as provide other services, such as deep conditioning treatments, special-occasion long-hair designs, and a variety of hair-addition techniques.

A licensed hairstylist can perform the hair services noted above and is also trained and licensed to do the basics of esthetics and nail technology. To specialize in esthetics or nail technology, additional courses are taken in each of these disciplines—or someone can study just esthetics or just nail technology and get a license in either or both of these areas.

Cosmetology schools teach some aspects of human physiology and anatomy, including the bone structure of the head and some elementary facts about the nervous system, in addition to hair skills. Some schools have now added psychology-related courses, dealing with people skills and communications.

Hairstylists may be employed in shops that have as few as one or two employees, or as many as 20 or more. They may work in privately owned salons or in a salon that is part of a large or small chain of beauty shops. They may work in hotels, department stores, hospitals, nursing homes, and resort areas, or on cruise ships. In recent years, a number of hair professionals—especially in big cities—have gone to work in larger facilities, sometimes known as spas or institutes, which offer a variety of health and beauty services. One such business, for example, offers complete hair design/treatment/color services; manicures and pedicures; makeup; bridal services; spa services including different kinds of facials (thermal mask, anti-aging, acne treatment), body treatments (exfoliating sea salt glow, herbal body wrap), scalp treatments, hydrotherapy water treatments, massage therapy, eyebrow/eyelash tweezing and tinting, and hair-removal treatments for all parts of the body; a fashion boutique; and even a wellness center staffed with board-certified physicians.

Those who operate their own shops must also take care of the details of business operations. Bills must be paid, orders placed, invoices and supplies checked, equipment serviced, and records and books kept. The selection, hiring, and termination of other workers are also the owner's responsibility. Like other responsible businesspeople, shop and salon owners are likely to be asked to participate in civic and community projects and activities.

Some stylists work for cosmetic/hair product companies. Sean Woodyard, for instance, in addition to being employed as a stylist at a big-city salon, teaches hair coloring for a major national cosmetics/hair care company. When the company introduces a new product or sells an existing product to a new salon, the company hires hair professionals as "freelance educators" to teach the stylists at the salon how to use the product. Woodyard has traveled all over the country during the past six years, while still keeping his full-time job, teaching color techniques at salons, and also participating in demonstrations for the company at trade shows. "I've taught all levels of classes," he says, "from a very basic color demonstration to a very complex color correction class. I've also been responsible for training other educators. I have really enjoyed traveling to other locales and having the opportunity to see other salons and other parts of the beauty and fashion industry."

At industry shows, his activities are varied. Woodyard is representing the company, "whether I'm standing behind a booth selling products or working on stage, demonstrating the product, or assisting a guest artist backstage, doing prep work. This has given me a real hands-on education, and I've been able to work with some of the top hair stylists in the country."

Woodyard has been working, as he says, "behind the chair" for 14 years. His first job after graduating from cosmetology school was at a small barber shop in his hometown. From there, he moved on to a larger salon, and then on to work in a big city. "Work behind the chair led me to want to do color," he says. "This really interested me. I guess wanting to know more about it myself is the reason why I researched it and became so involved with color. As I learned more about hair coloring, I became competent and more confident." The challenge, he says is to learn the "laws of color": how to choose a shade to get a specific result on a client's hair. He is now considered a color expert and is the head of the chemical department at his salon. "I've always been involved some way in outside education," Woodyard notes. "I've never been in a job where I have just worked 40 hours behind the chair. I've always been involved in some kind of training. I like to share what I know."

Cosmetologists must know how to market themselves to build their business. Whether they are self-employed or work for a salon or company, they are in business for themselves. It is the cosmetologist's skills and personality that will attract or fail to attract clients to that particular cosmetologist's chair. A marketing strategy Woodyard uses is to give several of his business cards to each of his clients. When one of his clients recommends him to a prospective new client, he gives both the old and new client a discount on a hair service.

Karol Thousand is the managing director of corporate school operations for a large cosmetology school that has four campuses in metropolitan areas in two states. She began as a stylist employed by salons and then owned her own shop for seven years. Her business was in an area that was destroyed by a tornado. It was then that she looked at different opportunities to decide the direction of her career. "I looked at the business end of the profession," she says, "and I took some additional business courses, and was then introduced to the school aspect of the profession. I have a passion for the beauty business and as I explored various training programs, I thought to myself, 'Hey, this is something I'd like to do!'"

Thousand managed a cosmetology school in Wisconsin before moving to Chicago for her current position. She says, "This is an empowering and satisfying profession. Not only do you make someone look better, but 99 percent of the time, they will feel better about themselves. In cosmetology, you can have the opportunity several times a day to help change the total look and perspective of an individual."

Cosmetologists serving the public must have pleasant, friendly, yet professional attitudes, as well as skill, ability, and an interest in their craft. These qualities are necessary in building a following of steady customers. The nature of their work requires cosmetologists to be aware of the psychological aspects of dealing with all types of personalities. Sometimes this can require diplomacy skills and a high degree of tolerance in dealing with different clients.

"To me," Sean Woodyard admits, "doing hair is just as much about self-gratification as it is about pleasing the client. It makes me feel good to make somebody else look good and feel good. It's also, of course, a great artistic and creative outlet."

Requirements

HIGH SCHOOL

High school students interested in the cosmetology field can help build a good foundation for postsecondary training by taking subjects in the areas of art, science (especially a basic chemistry course), health, business, and communication arts. Psychology and speech courses could also be helpful.

POSTSECONDARY TRAINING

To become a licensed cosmetologist, you must have completed an undergraduate course of a certain number of classroom credit hours. The required number varies from state to state—anywhere from 1,050 to

2,200 hours. (For example, Illinois requires 1,500, Iowa 2,100, and Wisconsin 1,600.) The program takes from 10 to 24 months to complete, again depending on the state. Evening courses are also frequently offered, and these take two to four months longer to complete. Applicants must also pass a written test, and in some states, an oral test, before they receive a license. Most states will allow a cosmetologist to work as an apprentice until the license is received, which normally involves just a matter of weeks.

A 1,500-hour undergraduate course at a cosmetology school in Illinois is typical of schools around the country. The program consists of theoretical and practical instruction divided into individual units of learning. Students are taught through the media of theory, audiovisual presentation, lectures, demonstrations, practical hands-on experiences, and written and practical testing. All schools have what they call clinic areas or floors, where people can have their hair done (or avail themselves of esthetics or nail services) by students at a discounted price, compared to what they would pay in a regular shop or salon.

One course, "Scientific Approach to Hair Sculpture," teaches students how to sculpt straight and curly hair, ethnic and Caucasian, using shears, texturizing tools and techniques, razors, and electric clippers. Teaching tools include mannequins, slip-ons, hair wefts, rectangles, and profiles. People skills segments are part of each course. Among other courses are "Scientific Approach to Perm Design," "Systematic Approach to Color," and "Systematic Approach to Beauty Care." Three different salon prep courses focus on retailing, business survival skills, and practical applications for contemporary design. The program concludes with final testing as well as extensive reviews and preparations for state board testing through the mock state board written practical examination.

Karol Thousand notes that, at her school and others throughout the country, "Twenty-five years ago, the courses focused mainly on technical skills. This is still the core focus, but now we teach more interpersonal skills. Our People Skills program helps students understand the individual, the different personality types—to better comprehend how they fit in and how to relate to their clients. We also teach sales and marketing skills—how to sell themselves and their services and products, as well as good business management skills."

Some states offer student internship programs. One such program that was recently initiated in Illinois aims to send better-prepared students/junior stylists into the workforce upon completion of their training from a licensed school. This program allows students to enter into a work-study program for 10 percent of their training in either cosmetology, esthetics, or nail technology. The state requires a student to complete at least 750 hours of training prior to making application for the program.

The program allows a student to experience firsthand the expectations of a salon, to perform salon services to be evaluated by their supervisor, and to experience different types of salon settings. The participating salons have the opportunity to prequalify potential employees before they graduate and work with the school regarding the skill levels of the student interns. This will also enhance job placement programs already in place in the school. The state requires that each participating salon be licensed and registered with the appropriate state department and file proof of registration with the school, along with the name and license number of their cosmetologist who is assigned to supervise students, before signing a contract or agreement.

CERTIFICATION OR LICENSING

At the completion of the proper number of credit hours, students must pass a formal examination before they can be licensed. The exam takes just a few hours. Some states also require a practical (hands-on) test and oral exams. Most, however, require just written tests. State Board Examinations are given at regular intervals. After about a month, test scores are available. Those who have passed then send in a licensure application and a specified fee to the appropriate state department. It takes about four to six weeks for a license to be issued.

Temporary permits are issued in most states, allowing students who have passed the test and applied for a license to practice their profession while they wait to receive the actual license. Judy Vargas, manager of the professional services section of the Illinois Department of Professional Regulation, warns students not to practice without a temporary permit or a license. "This is the biggest violation we see," she says, "and there are penalties of up to $1,000 per violation."

Graduate courses on advanced techniques and new methods and styles are also available at many cosmetology schools. Many states require licensed cosmetologists to take a specified number of credit hours, called continuing-education units, or CEUs. Illinois, for instance, requires each licensed cosmetologist to complete 10 to 14 CEUs each year. Licenses must be renewed in all states, generally every year or every two years.

In the majority of states, the minimum age for an individual to obtain a cosmetology license is 16. Because standards and requirements vary from state to state, students are urged to contact the licensing board of the state in which they plan to be employed.

OTHER REQUIREMENTS

Hairstyles change from season to season. As a cosmetologist, you should realize you will need to keep up with current fashion trends and often be learning new procedures to create new looks. You should be able to visualize different styles and make suggestions to your clients about what is best for them. And even if you don't specialize in coloring hair, you should have a good sense of color. One of your most important responsibilities will be to make your clients feel comfortable around you and happy with their looks. To do this, you will need to develop both your talking and listening skills.

Exploring

Talk to friends or parents of friends who are working in the industry, or just go to a local salon or cosmetology school and ask questions about the profession. Go to the library and get books on careers in the beauty/hair care industry. Search the Internet for related Web sites. Individuals with an interest in the field might seek after-school or summer employment as a general shop helper in a barber shop or a salon. Some schools may permit potential students to visit and observe classes.

Employers

The most common employers of hairstylists are, of course, beauty salons. However, hairstylists also find work at department stores, hospitals, nursing homes, spas, resorts, cruise ships, and cosmetics companies. The demand for services in the cosmetology field—hairstyling in particular—far exceeds the supply; additionally, the number of salons increases by 2 percent each year. Considering that most cosmetology schools have placement services to assist graduates, finding employment usually is not difficult for most cosmetologists. As with most jobs in the cosmetology field, opportunities will be concentrated in highly populated areas; however, there will be jobs available for hairstylists virtually everywhere. Many hairstylists/cosmetologists aspire ultimately to be self-employed. This can be a rewarding avenue if one has plenty of experience and good business sense (not to mention start-up capital or financial backing); it also requires long hours and a great deal of hard work.

Starting Out

To be a licensed cosmetologist/hairstylist, you must graduate from an accredited school and pass a state test. Once that is accomplished, you can apply for jobs that are advertised in the newspapers or over the Internet, or apply at an employment agency specializing in these professions. Most schools have placement services to help their graduates find jobs. Some salons have training programs from which they hire new employees.

Scholarships or grants that can help you pay for your schooling are available. One such program is the Access to Cosmetology Education (ACE) Grant. It is sponsored by the American Association of Cosmetology Schools (AACS), the Beauty and Barber Supply Institute Inc., and the Cosmetology Advancement Foundation. Interested students can find out about ACE Grants and obtain applications at participating schools, salons, and distributors or through these institutions. The criteria for receiving an ACE Grant include approval from an AACS member school, recommendations from two salons, and a high school diploma or GED.

Advancement

Individuals in the beauty/hair care industry most frequently begin by working at a shop or salon. Many aspire to be self-employed and own their own shops. There are many factors to consider when contemplating going into business on one's own. Usually it is essential to obtain experience and financial capital before seeking to own a shop. The cost of equipping even a one-chair shop can be very high. Owning a large shop or a chain of shops is an aspiration for the very ambitious.

Some pursue advanced educational training in one aspect of beauty culture, such as hairstyling or coloring. Others who are more interested in the business aspects can take courses in business management skills and move into shop or salon management, or work for a corporation related to the industry. Manufacturers and distributors frequently have exciting positions available for those with exceptional talent and creativity. Cosmetologists work on the stage as platform artists, or take some additional education courses and teach at a school of cosmetology.

Some schools publish their own texts and other printed materials for students. They want people who have cosmetology knowledge and experience as well as writing skills to write and edit these materials. An artistic director for the publishing venue of one large school has a cosmetology degree in addition to degrees in art. Other cosmetologists might design hairstyles for fashion magazines, industry publications, fashion shows, television presentations, or movies. They might get involved in the political end of the business, such as working for a state licensing board. There are many and varied career possibilities cosmetologists can explore in the beauty/hair care industry.

Earnings

Cosmetologists can make an excellent living in the beauty/hair care industry, but as in most careers, they don't receive very high pay when just starting out. Though their raise in salary may start slowly, the curve quickly escalates. The U.S. Department of Labor reports cosmetologists and hairstylists had a median annual income (including tips) of $17,660 in 2000. The lowest paid 10 percent, which generally included those beginning in the profession, made less than $12,280. The highest paid 10 percent earned more than $33,220. Again, both those salaries include tips. On the extreme upward end of the pay scale, some fashion stylists in New York or Hollywood charge $300 per haircut! Their annual salary can go into six figures. Salaries in larger cities are greater than those in smaller towns, but then the cost of living is higher in the big cities, too.

Most shops and salons give a new employee a guaranteed income instead of commission. If the employee goes over the guaranteed amount, then he or she earns a commission. Usually, this guarantee will extend for the first three months of employment, so that the new stylist can focus on building up business before going on straight commission.

In addition, most salon owners grant incentives for product sales; and, of course, there are always tips. However, true professionals never depend on their tips. If a stylist receives a tip, it's a nice surprise for a job well done, but it's good business practice not to expect these bonuses. All tips must be recorded and reported to the Internal Revenue Service.

The benefits a cosmetologist receives, such as health insurance and retirement plans, depend on the place of employment. A small independent salon cannot afford to supply a hefty benefit package, but a large shop or salon or a member of a chain can be more generous. However, some of the professional associations and organizations offer benefit packages at reasonable rates.

Work Environment

Those employed in the cosmetology industry usually work a five- or six-day week, which averages approximately 40 to 50 hours. Weekends and days preceding holidays may be especially busy. Cosmetologists are on their feet a lot and are usually working in a small space. Strict sanitation codes must be observed in all shops and salons, and they are comfortably heated, ventilated, and well lighted.

Hazards of the trade include nicks and cuts from scissors and razors, minor burns when care is not used in handling hot towels or instruments, and occasional skin irritations arising from constant use of grooming aids that contain chemicals. Some of the chemicals used in hair dyes or permanent solutions can be very abrasive; plastic gloves are required for handling and contact. Pregnant women are advised to avoid contact with many of the chemicals present in hair products.

Stylists employed in department store salons will have more of a guaranteed client flow, with more walk-ins from people who are shopping. A freestanding salon might have a more predictable pace, with more scheduled appointments and fewer walk-ins.

Stylist Sean Woodyard says, "I've always enjoyed the atmosphere of a salon. There's constant action and something different happening every day. A salon attracts artistic, creative people, and the profession allows me to be part of the fashion industry."

Some may find it difficult to work constantly in such close, personal contact with the public at large, especially when they strive to satisfy customers who are difficult to please or disagreeable. The work demands an even temperament, a pleasant disposition, and patience.

Outlook

The future looks good for cosmetology. According to the U.S. Department of Labor, employment should grow about as fast as the average through 2010. Our growing population, the availability of disposable income, and changes in hair fashion that are practically seasonal all contribute to the demand for cosmetologists. In addition, turnover in this career is fairly high as cosmetologists move up into management positions, change careers, or leave the field for other reasons. Competition for jobs at higher-paying, prestigious salons, however, is strong.

For More Information

Contact the following organizations for more information on cosmetology careers:
AMERICAN ASSOCIATION OF COSMETOLOGY SCHOOLS
15825 North 71st Street, Suite 100
Scottsdale, AZ 85254-1521
Tel: 800-831-1086
Web: http://www.beautyschools.org

BEAUTY AND BARBER SUPPLY INSTITUTE, INC.
15825 North 71st Street, Suite 100
Scottsdale, AZ 85254
Tel: 800-468-2274
Web: http://www.bbsi.org

NATIONAL ACCREDITING COMMISSION OF COSMETOLOGY ARTS AND SCIENCES
4401 Ford Avenue, Suite 1300
Arlington, VA 22302-1432
Tel: 703-600-7600
Web: http://www.naccas.org

NATIONAL COSMETOLOGY ASSOCIATION
401 North Michigan Avenue
Chicago, IL 60611
Tel: 312-527-6765
Web: http://www.salonprofessionals.org

For fun facts on hairstyling, visit the following Web site:
HAIR INTERNATIONAL
Web: http://www.hairinternational.com

Dermatologists

Overview

Dermatologists study, diagnose, and treat diseases and ailments of the skin, hair, mucous membranes, nails, and related tissues or structures. They may also perform cosmetic services, such as scar removal or hair transplants. There are approximately 598,000 physicians of all types working in the United States. According to the American Medical Association, approximately 1.2 percent specialize in dermatology.

History

Many in the medical profession opposed specialization when it began to occur in the 19th century. They thought treatments would be too fragmented for patients' own good. There were several factors, however, that made specialization inevitable. The amount of medical information was increasing, and complex new techniques were developing at such a rapid pace that doctors could not keep up with the advances. They began to send patients to physicians who concentrated on one type of illness or manipulation. Specialization was also attractive because it gave doctors the opportunity to demand higher fees, work fewer hours, and command greater respect from peers and the public. Medical experts gradually abandoned their ideas that general disease was caused by generalized problems and began to diagnose and treat local organs instead.

The specialty of dermatology had its beginnings in the mid-1800s in Vienna when a doctor named Ferdinand von Hebra, one of the first to specialize entirely in skin diseases, founded a division of dermatology. At that time, medicine concentrated primarily on abnormalities in the four humors, or elemental fluids of the body—blood, phlegm, black bile, and yellow bile—and they believed symptoms were caused by those abnormalities. Hebra made classifications based on changes in the tissues instead of on symptoms or on general disease categories. As a result, his treatment was directed toward the local problem rather than treating imbalances in the humors. He was responsible for the discovery that scabies was transmissible from person to person and could be cured by the destruction of the itch-mite parasite.

Dermatologists use magnifying lenses to view the skin up close. Innumerable discoveries have been made, including new medicines, treatments, and equipment. Lasers and computer technology, for example, have drastically changed dermatology, improving diagnostic techniques and allowing certain surgical procedures to be performed without using a scalpel.

The Job

Dermatologists study, diagnose, and treat diseases and ailments of the largest, most visible organ of the body, the skin, and its related tissues and structures—hair, mucous membranes, and nails. Their work begins with diagnosis to determine the cause of the disease or condition. This process involves studying a patient's history, conducting visual examinations, and taking blood samples, smears of the affected skin, microscopic scrapings, or biopsy specimens of the skin. They may order cultures of fungi or bacteria or perform patch and photosensitivity tests to reveal allergies and immunologic diseases. They may also evaluate bone marrow, lymph nodes, and endocrine glands. Usually dermatologists send skin, tissue, or blood specimens to a laboratory for chemical and biological testing and analysis.

Dermatologists treat some skin problems with prescribed oral medications, such as antibiotics, or topical applications. Certain types of eczema and dermatitis, psoriasis, acne, or impetigo can usually be treated with creams, ointments, or oral medicines.

Exposure to ultraviolet light is used to treat such conditions as psoriasis, and radiation therapy is occasionally used to treat keloids (scar tissue that grows excessively).

Some skin conditions and illnesses require surgical treatment. There are three types of skin cancer—basal cell carcinoma, squamous cell carcinoma, and malignant melanoma—which must be removed surgically. Dermatologists may use traditional surgery, where the cancerous cells and surrounding tissue are cut away, but some cancers can be removed by lasers, frozen by cryosurgery, destroyed with a cautery device (high-frequency electric current), or destroyed by radiation therapy. Another type of surgery dermatologists use is Moh's surgery, in which progressive layers of skin and tissue are cut out and examined microscopically for the presence of cancers. Dermatologists also perform skin graft procedures to repair wounds that are too large to be stitched together. After removal of a skin tumor, for example, they take a portion of skin from another part of the patient's body, such as the thigh, and attach it to the wound. Since the skin graft comes from the patient's own body, there is no problem with rejection.

Not all surgeries that dermatologists perform are major. There are many conditions that can be treated with simple outpatient procedures under local anesthetic, including removal of warts, sebaceous cysts, scars, moles, cosmetic defects of the skin, boils, and abscesses. Hair transplants are usually done in the doctor's office, as are laser treatments for disfiguring birth defects, cysts, birthmarks, spider veins, and growths.

Certain diseases can manifest themselves in a skin condition. When dermatologists see that a skin problem is a sign of an illness in another part of the patient's body, they recommend treatment by other specialists. If a patient complains of itchy or scaly skin, for example, it may be an allergy. Boils may be a sign of diabetes mellitus, and a skin rash may indicate secondary syphilis. Dermatologists must often consult with allergists, internists, and other doctors. In turn, many dermatologists are called on by other specialists to help diagnose complicated symptoms.

Dermatologists deal not only with the physical aspects of skin afflictions, but the emotional aspects, too. Patients often have to face embarrassment, ridicule, and rejection because of their skin ailments, and dermatologists can help them overcome this kind of trauma.

Within the field of dermatology there are some subspecialties. *Dermatoimmunologists* focus on the treatment of diseases that involve the immune system, including allergies. They may use a procedure called immunofluorescence to diagnose and characterize these skin disorders. *Dermatopathologists* study the tissue structure and features of skin diseases. *Dermatologic surgeons* perform Moh's micrographic surgery and cosmetic procedures, including collagen injections, sclerotherapy (the injection of varicose veins with a fluid), and dermabrasion (a planing of the skin using sandpaper, wire brushes, or other abrasive materials). *Pediatric dermatologists* treat skin disorders in children. *Occupational dermatologists* study and treat occupational disorders, such as forms of dermatitis from chemical or biological irritants.

Some dermatologists combine a private practice with a teaching position at a medical school. Others are involved in research, developing new treatments, and finding cures for skin ailments. A few work in industry, developing cosmetics, lotions, and other consumer products.

Requirements

HIGH SCHOOL
Dermatologists, like all physicians, have completed a great deal of education. You should realize that after high school your education will continue on through college, medical school, and a residency in your specialty. In high school you can start preparing for both college and your medical studies by taking science classes such as biology, chemistry, physics, and anatomy. Mathematics classes, such as algebra and geometry, will give you experience in working with numbers and formulas, both important skills for this career. Make sure your high school education is well rounded and college preparatory by taking English and history classes as well as a foreign language. Also, psychology classes and other social science classes may give you a background in understanding people—an important skill for any doctor. Take this time to develop your study habits and determine how well you like the course of study.

POSTSECONDARY TRAINING
Your next step after high school is to earn a bachelor's degree, typically with a major in a science field such as biology or chemistry, from an accredited four-year college. Some schools may offer well-defined premedical courses of study, while others will allow you to structure your own education. In either case, your college studies should concentrate on the sciences, including biology, physics, organic chemistry, and inorganic chemistry. In addition, you should continue to take mathematics, English, and social science courses. Language classes, particular Latin, may help you in your medical school studies.

While you are in your second or third year of college, you should arrange with an advisor to take the Medical College Admission Test (MCAT). All medical colleges in this country require this test for admission. After you receive your undergraduate degree, you can apply to one of the 144 medical schools in the United States. The admissions process is terribly competitive and includes evaluation by a committee that considers grade point averages, MCAT scores, and recommendations from professors. Most premedical students apply to several medical schools long before graduation, and only about one-third of all applicants are accepted. Medical school study and training lasts four years, at the end of which you will earn the degree of Doctor of Medicine (M.D.).

For the first two years of medical school, you will attend lectures and classes and spend time in laboratories. Courses include anatomy, biochemistry, physiology, pharmacology, psychology, microbiology, pathology, medical ethics, and laws governing medicine. Medical students learn to take patient histories, perform examinations, and recognize symptoms. In their third and fourth years, medical students are involved in more practical studies. They work in clinics and hospitals supervised by physicians learning acute, chronic, preventive, and rehabilitative care. They go through rotations in internal medicine, family practice, obstetrics and gynecology, pediatrics, psychiatry, and surgery in which they practice and learn the skills of diagnosing and treating illnesses.

After medical school, all physicians must pass an examination given by the National Board of Medical Examiners in order to receive a license from the state in which they intend to practice. Most physicians then begin their residency to learn a specialty. Only about half of the applicants for the accredited residency programs in the United States are accepted, and dermatology is very competitive.

Residency training for dermatologists lasts a minimum of four years, three of which are spent specializing in dermatology. The first year is a clinical residency program in internal medicine, family practice, general surgery, or pediatrics. The next three years are spent studying and practicing dermatology. Residents are closely supervised as they study skin pathology, bacteriology, radiology, surgery, biochemistry, allergy and immunology, and other basics. Intensive laboratory work in mycology (the study of the fungi that infect humans) is usually required. Following the residency, dermatologists can become certified by the American Board of Dermatology and have full professional standing.

CERTIFICATION OR LICENSING

Certification in dermatology, as mentioned above, is given by the American Board of Dermatology. Although certification is voluntary, it is strongly recommended. Certification demonstrates the physician's dedication to the field, assures patients of his or her educational qualifications, and affirms that the physician has met the American Board of Dermatology's standards to practice this specialty. To qualify for certification, you must have completed your residency and pass written and sometimes practical examinations given by the American Board of Dermatology. Certification is for a period of ten years. Even after 11 years of study, dermatologists must continue to study throughout their careers in order to keep up with medical advances and retain board certification.

All physicians in the United States must be licensed to practice. Some states have reciprocity agreements with other states so that a physician licensed in one state may be automatically licensed in another without being required to pass another examination.

OTHER REQUIREMENTS

Medical school and the dermatological residency are filled with stress and pressure, and they are also physically demanding. Residents often work 24-hour shifts and put in 80 hours a week or more. They need to be emotionally stable in order to handle the stress of this intense schedule. Physicians need self-confidence because they make decisions on critical medical issues. They must also have keen observation skills, be detail oriented, and have excellent memories. Finally, because this is a "people job," physicians need to be able to relate to people with compassion and understanding.

Exploring

You may be able to schedule a time at a dermatologist's office for a tour of the facilities. When making the appointment, explain that you are interested in a dermatology career and ask if you could set up an informational interview with the doctor. Go to the interview prepared with questions about topics that concern you. What, for example, was the most difficult aspect of the schooling? What are the most rewarding aspects of the work? What advice would the doctor give to someone interested in pursuing this career?

If you are unable to visit a dermatologist's office, try to tour other medical settings such as hospitals, clinics, and health care facilities. Talk to your family doctor about the field of medicine in general and explain your interest. Your family doctor may have contacts who would be happy to speak to you.

You should certainly try to do volunteer work in a hospital, a clinic, or even a nursing home. Volunteer work will give you exposure to a health care environment and practical experience and allow you to gauge how well you like working in the medical field. In addition, such experience will add to your credentials when you apply to college and medical school.

Employers

Most dermatologists are in private practice, either individually or with others. A few work for hospitals or similar health agencies. Some establish their practices at large university medical centers in order to combine an active practice with teaching at a university or medical school. Researchers work in university or private laboratories searching for new cures and treatments.

Starting Out

Once a doctor finishes the residency program, there are several options for beginning to practice dermatology. The most difficult is to set up a private practice. It is a considerable expense to purchase the necessary equipment and supplies, pay staff salaries, rent office space, pay liability insurance, and advertise. It can take up to 15 years to become established and reach full earning potential.

A second option is to take over the practice of a dermatologist who is retiring or relocating. This has the benefit of offering an already existing patient list.

Some dermatologists join a group practice or enter into partnership with a related medical specialist such as an allergist, an immunologist, or a plastic surgeon.

Many newly qualified dermatologists are much more likely to take salaried jobs in group medical practices, clinics, or health maintenance organizations. After several years, they may decide to open their own practices. Some find opportunities with federal or state agencies, private businesses, or the military.

Advancement

Dermatologists with their own private practices can increase their earnings or improve their clinical status by expanding their practices or moving to larger cities. They may become teachers at medical schools in addition to treating patients, or they may go into research.

Some go into hospital administration, where they have less contact with patients and more involvement with staff and the day-to-day operation of the hospital.

Many physicians participate in national organizations—such as the American Medical Association or the American Academy of Dermatology—where they can serve on committees and be elected to offices, increasing their status.

Earnings

The American Medical Association reports that the median annual salary (after expenses) for all physicians was approximately $160,000 in 1998. The association also reports that the middle 50 percent of physicians made between $120,000 and $240,000. Earnings, however, are affected by specialty, number of years in practice, geographic region, hours worked, and the skill, personality, and professional standing of the doctor.

According to *Physicians Compensation Survey*, published by the recruiting agency Physicians Search, dermatologists in their first year of practice earned an average salary of $150,000 in 2001, and salaries ranged from $120,000 to $200,000. Dermatologists who had been practicing more than three years earned an average of $232,000. Salaries ranged from $168,988 to $407,000.

Dermatologists in private practice or group partnerships have the potential for higher earnings, but they must cover all of their own business expenses and benefits. For those hired by health care organizations, in addition to salary, dermatologists may receive benefits, including health and life insurance, malpractice liability insurance, paid vacation, and retirement plans. Some earn productivity bonuses as well.

Work Environment

Dermatologists are often solo practitioners. They work in well-lighted, air-conditioned offices, and they are usually assisted by clerical and nursing staff. A certain number of hours are spent each week visiting patients at the hospital. Most dermatologists also spend some time in laboratory settings, either their own or in a hospital. Most specialists, including dermatologists, work in large urban areas.

Working hours are usually regular, since dermatologists see patients by appointment in their offices. They schedule surgeries and follow-up visits both at their offices and at hospitals. Dermatologists occasionally may have to answer emergency calls, such as to treat burn victims.

Dermatologists work 40 to 50 hours a week, mostly during normal daytime hours, though some work up to 60 hours a week. They often try to accommodate the working schedules of their patients by opening their offices on Saturdays or one evening a week.

Outlook

The health care industry is thriving, and the U.S. Department of Labor predicts employment for physicians to grow as fast as the average through 2010. The field of dermatology is expected to expand for a number of reasons. New technologies, medicines, and treatments continue to be developed at a rapid pace. Another factor in the growth of this industry is that the population is growing and aging, requiring more skin-related health care in advancing years. Demand for dermatologists has increased as people have become aware of the effects of radiation exposure from the sun and of air pollutants on skin. The public is also much more aware of the benefits of good general and dermatological health.

For More Information

The AAD offers information on dermatological conditions, employment opportunities, and professional concerns. Visit the AAD Web site for information on dermatology for young children.
AMERICAN ACADEMY OF DERMATOLOGY (AAD)
930 North Meacham Road
Schaumburg, IL 60173-4927
Web: http://www.aad.org

For information on certification and other career materials, contact:
AMERICAN BOARD OF DERMATOLOGY
Henry Ford Hospital
I Ford Place
Detroit, MI 48202-3450
Tel: 313-874-1088
Web: http://www.abderm.org

For more information on the medical profession in general and about certain medical conditions, check out the following Web site:
AMERICAN MEDICAL ASSOCIATION
515 North State Street
Chicago, IL 60610
Tel: 312-464-5000
Web: http://www.ama-assn.org

Electrologists

Quick Facts

School Subjects
  Biology
  Health
Personal Skills
  Helping/teaching
  Mechanical/manipulative
Work Environment
  Primarily indoors
  Primarily one location
Minimum Education Level
  Some postsecondary training
Salary Range
  $17,660 to $20,080 to $65,000
Certification or Licensing
  Required by certain states
Outlook
  About as fast as the average

Overview

Electrologists are trained professionals who are charged with removing hair from the skin of patients. The electrologist uses a probe to shoot an electric wave into the papilla, or root, of the hair to kill the root and deter new hair growth. Since the root may not be destroyed on the first try, it is often necessary to treat the same area many times over a period of months or even years.

History

Since many people today find excess facial or body hair unattractive, numerous convenient and affordable methods of hair removal are available. Depilatories are sometimes used to dissolve the hair, but they have the potential to irritate the skin and often have unpleasant odors. Shaving, or cutting the hair close to the skin with a blade or razor (one of the most popular methods of controlling body hair), can lead to skin cuts, chafing, and ingrown hairs. With waxing, a warm wax is applied to the area where hair is to be removed. A piece of cloth is then placed on the wax and ripped off quickly, ripping out the attached hairs. Sugaring is based on the same principle, but it is said to be safer since it uses a cool solution instead of hot wax. Both sugaring and waxing can lead to increased skin sensitivity and ingrown hairs. With tweezing, the hairs are plucked individually with small forceps. This is usually more effective for small, delicate areas of the body, such as the eyebrow area, where other hair removal techniques might be dangerous or less effective. Shaving, sugaring, waxing, and tweezing have all been used to provide temporary solutions for hairiness, but these methods only cut or temporarily remove the hair; they do nothing to prevent future growth. Electrolysis is the only method reported to remove unwanted hair permanently, and when performed by a professional electrologist, it can be safer than many chemical products and other treatments.

The practice of electrology began in 1869, when Dr. Charles E. Michel, a Missouri ophthalmologist, used a probe and electric current to remove ingrown eyelashes for his patients. In the early 1900s, the multiple-needle technique for galvanic electrolysis was developed. Around the same time, Dr. Henri Bordier, of Lyon, France, developed the method of thermolysis, or electrolysis, using short waves and a high frequency. Improvements throughout the years have led to safer treatments. A current trend in electrology is the development and use of computerized equipment that delivers a safer and more reliable electrical charge. Disposable needles and other materials are also becoming the norm. Improvements in equipment and more stringent standardization procedures for certification of machinery and operators are making electrolysis safer and more accessible to all.

The Job

Electrologists, who usually conduct business in a professional office, salon, or medical clinic, work with only one patron at a time. This enables them to focus their complete attention and concentration on the delicate treatment they are performing. Since electrolysis can sometimes be uncomfortable, it reassures patrons to know that the practitioner's complete focus is on them and their needs. A high level of professionalism helps patients put their trust in the electrologist and may make them more receptive to the treatment.

Electrologists often begin their work with a personal consultation. It is essential for electrologists to interview potential clients to understand why they want to have the hair removed and what expectations they have about the procedure. The electrologist should explain the process in detail, discussing possible side effects as well as the effectiveness and duration of individual sessions and approximate length of time before the treatments are complete. A good electrologist also may suggest alternate methods of hair removal that may be more cost effective or appropriate for different clients and their needs.

Before beginning a session, the electrologist needs to make sure that the areas to be treated and all instruments used are sterile. A sanitary work environment is crucial for the safety of the electrologist as well as the person undergoing treatment. The electrologist may have an assistant or trainee help with these preparations. The first step in the treatment session is the cleansing of the area of skin that will be treated. Rubbing alcohol or an antiseptic is often used for this purpose. Once the skin is cleansed, hair removal can begin. Electrologists use a round-tipped probe to enter the opening of the skin fold, also known as the hair follicle. The probe also penetrates the papilla, which is the organ beneath the hair root. The electrologist sets the proper amount and duration of the electrical current in advance and presses gently on a floor pedal to distribute that current through the probe. The electrical current helps deaden the tissue, after which the hair can be lifted out gently with a pair of tweezers or forceps.

Electrologists determine the extent of treatments that will be necessary for complete removal of the unwanted hair. They may schedule weekly appointments that last 15, 30, 45, or even 60 minutes. The length of the individual appointments depends on both the amount of hair to be removed and the thickness and depth of the hair. Very coarse hair may take longer to treat, whereas fine hair may be permanently removed in only a few sessions. If a patient is very sensitive to the treatments, the electrologist may set up shorter appointments or schedule more time between sessions. Some electrologists use a gold needle on sensitive clients to minimize adverse reactions, which can include itching, bumps, redness, and pustules. Most of these reactions can be treated with topical ointments and proper skin care.

Electrologists can remove hair from almost any area of the body. The most common areas they treat are the arms, legs, chest, and portions of the face such as upper or lower lip, chin, or cheek. Electrologists should not remove hair from inside the ears or nose or from the eyelids. They should also have the written consent of a physician to remove hair from a mole or birthmark. As with many professions, electrologists should have legitimate malpractice insurance coverage.

As with all cosmetic treatments, the procedure can be fairly expensive. Since electrolysis is performed mainly for esthetic reasons, it is generally not covered by any health insurance plans. Also, electrolysis is not a "quick fix." Constant maintenance is necessary for some clients, and people often have electrolysis treatments for years in certain areas before the hair root is finally destroyed.

Requirements

HIGH SCHOOL

While you are in high school you should take classes in science, anatomy, physiology, and health if you are interested in pursuing a career as an electrologist. These classes will give you a good understanding of the human body and its functions. Learning about hair and how it grows, in addition to the theories and practices of electrology, can help a potential electrologist decide if this is the proper career path for him or her. In addition, you should consider taking classes in communications, psychology, and bookkeeping, accounting, or business management. These classes will give you skills for working well with people as well as help you if you decide to establish your own practice.

POSTSECONDARY TRAINING

Once you have gotten your high school diploma or equivalency certificate, you can enroll in a trade school or professional school that offers electrolysis training. The quality of these programs may vary, so you should look for programs that offer courses of study in such areas as microbiology, dermatology, neurology, and electricity. You will also learn about proper sterilization and sanitation procedures to avoid infections or injury to yourself or your clients. Classes that cover cell composition, the endocrine system, the vascular pulmonary system, and basic anatomy will also be beneficial to you.

Although the training offered is designed to educate students about the theory of electrolysis and its relation to the skin and tissue, the greater part of the training is of a practical nature. You will spend many training hours learning the purpose and function of the different types of equipment. In addition, hands-on experience with patrons needing different treatments will give you confidence in operating equipment and working with people.

Programs may be offered on a full-time or part-time basis. Although tuition varies, some schools offer financial assistance or payment plans to make their programs more affordable. Sometimes lab and materials fees are charged. Check if the school you are interested in is accredited or associated with any professional organizations. Also, consider what state you want to work in after graduation. Licensing requirements of the various states may affect the length and type of training that the schools offer.

CERTIFICATION OR LICENSING

Certification, while voluntary, can indicate your commitment to the profession. A number of certification options are available. For example, the designation Certified Professional Electrologist (CPE) is offered by the American Electrology Association through the International Board of Electrologist Certification. The Society of Clinical and Medical Electrologists offers the title Certified Clinical Electrologist (CCE) through the National Commission for Electrologist Certification.

Some states require electrologists to be licensed. Those with this requirement offer the licensing examinations through their state health departments. The examination usually covers various topics in the areas of health and cosmetology. Most states require applicants for electrology licensing to have a minimum number of study hours and practical training. They must also pass a written theory examination, a state exam, and a clinical examination. You should become familiar with your state's licensing requirements prior to beginning your training so you can be sure your education provides you with everything necessary to practice.

OTHER REQUIREMENTS

Electrologists help people feel good about themselves by improving aspects of their physical appearance. People plagued by excess body hair see the procedure as a way for them to have a "normal" life, where they don't have to rely on temporary methods to remove hair or hide hairy areas. Electrologists feel a great sense of accomplishment for helping people through the various stages of their treatment and helping them to achieve their hair removal goals. They may sometimes feel the anxiety of a client who is impatient or unrealistic about the results or is nervous about the process. Because electrologists perform personal and sometimes uncomfortable treatments, it is important that they be patient and caring and develop an empathetic working style. A potential electrologist also should not be squeamish, since the procedure involves probes. Since the area to be treated is sometimes delicate, electrologists need to have good visual acuity and coordination to perform the procedures, although special accommodations may be made for practitioners with different abilities.

Exploring

To find out more about the field of electrology, try contacting local trade schools for information. Also, some two-year colleges that offer course work in medical technician careers may be able to supply you with literature on programs and training in electrology. If you are particularly interested in the field, make an appointment for an electrolysis consultation and perhaps pursue treatment for yourself.

Cosmetology schools, which are located in many different areas of the country, may also prove helpful for investigating this profession. Most schools and training programs allow interested students to speak with faculty and guidance counselors for further information. Ask if you can sit in on classes or contact a certified electrologist or patient of electrology to find out more about the field and procedures.

Employers

Electrologists are employed by salons, professional offices, and medical clinics, or they may be self-employed. In some cases, experienced electrologists may hire newly licensed electrologists as assistants.

Starting Out

Many electrologists begin as assistants to a practicing professional. These assistants may handle extra patients when the office is overbooked or have new patients referred to them. In this way, beginning electrologists can build a clientele without having to cover the high costs of equipment, supplies, and office space. Often, trade schools have job placement offices that help new electrologists build a practice. Also, some schools may offer alumni mentor programs, where the school introduces a new graduate to an established electrologist in order for both to benefit from each other. The new graduate can introduce new theories and practices to the professional and take care of overflow clients, while the professional can help the new electrologist build a client base and start his or her own practice.

Some electrologists may choose to open their own businesses in a medical office complex and receive referrals from their neighboring health care professionals. Electrologists are also employed by clinics or hospitals before they get their own office space. Beauty salons and health spas may have an electrologist on staff who can provide initial consultations with clients considering different methods of hair removal.

Advancement

Electrologists usually advance through building up the various aspects of their practices. As an electrologist becomes more experienced and gains a reputation, he or she often attracts more new patrons and repeat clients. Some electrologists who work as part of a clinic staff may open their own offices in a more visible and accessible location or office complex.

By obtaining additional training and education, electrologists can often branch out into other fields, including cosmetology and medicine. An electrologist trained in other methods may decide to offer clients additional hair removal procedures, such as waxing, sugaring, or laser hair removal. Electrologists can also become certified to teach the theory and practice of electrology in trade schools. Electrologists may also use their writing skills and practical experience to contribute to trade magazines, journals, and Web sites devoted to the field.

Earnings

Because electrologists schedule client treatments that vary in length, their fees are often based on quarter-hour appointments. Rates for a 15-minute treatment may begin at $15 in some cities, while charges in large urban regions may begin at $30. Treatments lasting 30 or 60 minutes in large cities may begin at $50 and $100, respectively. Although rates in smaller towns are often lower, electrologists there still earn a competitive wage for their work.

The *Occupational Outlook Handbook* reports the median yearly income for cosmetologists was $17,660 in 2000, and skin care specialists earned a median of $20,080. The American Electrology Association reports that full-time, established electrologists can earn between $35,000 and $65,000 per year. Electrologists who are employed by a medical clinic or salon may have to contribute a portion of their fees to help cover office space, utilities, and support staff such as receptionists and bookkeepers.

Electrologists employed by a salon or group practice generally get the same benefits as other employees, which may include health, dental, and life insurance, as well as disability coverage, retirement savings plans, and paid vacations. Self-employed electrologists usually must provide these things for themselves.

Work Environment

Whether the electrologist works in a professional office, a salon, a medical clinic, or a private shop, the nature of the work requires the environment to be clean, comfortable, and professional. Because electrologists perform delicate work, they may operate in spaces that are quiet to allow for greater concentration for the practitioner and to relax the client. Sometimes soothing music is played in the background to help put clients at ease.

A neat and professional appearance is important, so electrologists often wear uniforms or lab coats. As well as being comfortable and practical for the electrologist, a medical uniform may also reassure and comfort the client. Because of the threat of infectious diseases, electrologists may wear eye protection and disposable gloves during the procedure to reduce their risk of exposure. They also wash their hands frequently and maintain a sterile treatment area.

Electrologists generally spend most of their time in an office or treatment room, although not all that time is spent with clients. When not working on clients, electrologists may set up appointments, consult with prospective clients, train an assistant or future electrologist, or check equipment to ensure that it is functioning properly.

Outlook

The U.S. Department of Labor predicts job employment for those in the cosmetology field, which includes electrologists, to increase about as fast as the average through 2010. Many salons, professional offices, and hospitals and clinics are striving to offer cutting-edge technologies and services to maintain—or gain—a competitive edge, which will create more jobs for electrologists. Further, the demand for electrologists is growing due to the increased awareness of and interest in this service. There are generally greater opportunities for electrologists in larger cities and highly populated areas.

Since electrology has been in practice for over a century, many clients are feeling more comfortable with the procedure. Also, with more disposable income in families, people who once considered permanent hair removal a luxury are beginning to consider electrolysis a viable and affordable option.

For More Information

For information regarding the International Board of Electrologist Certification and for a directory of accredited schools and specific state requirements relating to electrology, contact:
AMERICAN ELECTROLOGY ASSOCIATION
106 Oakridge Road
Trumbull, CT 06611
Tel: 203-374-6667
Email: career@electrology.com
Web: http://www.electrology.com

For information on electrolysis and a list of guild members, contact:
INTERNATIONAL GUILD OF PROFESSIONAL ELECTROLOGISTS
803 North Main Street, Suite A
High Point, NC 27262
Tel: 800-830-3247
Email: info@igpe.org
Web: http://www.igpe.org

For career, certification, and education information, contact:
SOCIETY OF CLINICAL AND MEDICAL ELECTROLOGISTS, INC.
7600 Terrace Avenue, Suite 203
Middleton, WI 53562
Tel: 608-831-8009
Email: scme@guildassoc.com
Web: http://www.scmeweb.org

Makeup Artists

Overview

Makeup artists prepare actors for performances on stage and before cameras. They read scripts and consult with directors, producers, and technicians to design makeup effects for each individual character. They apply makeup and prosthetics and build and style wigs. They also create special makeup effects.

History

Theatrical makeup is as old as the theater itself. Cultures around the world performed ritualistic dances, designed by spiritual leaders, to communicate with gods and other supernatural forces. These dances often involved elaborate costumes and makeup. By the Elizabethan age, theater had become an entertainment requiring special makeup techniques to transform the male actors into female characters. In Asia in the 17th century, Kabuki theater maintained the symbolic origins of the drama; actors wore very stylized makeup to depict each character's nature and social standing. It wasn't until the late 18th century in Europe that plays, and therefore costumes and makeup, were based on realistic portrayals of society. The grease stick, a special makeup stick that could withstand harsh stage lights without smearing, was invented in the 19th century.

This grease stick led the way for other advancements in the chemistry of stage makeup, but even today's makeup artists must use ingenuity and invention to create special effects. With the advent of filmmaking came new challenges in makeup design—

artists were required to create makeup that would not only hold up under intense lighting, but would look realistic in close-up. The silent film star Lon Chaney was a pioneer in makeup effects; his dedication to the craft was so extreme that he permanently injured himself with the restrictive prosthetics he used in *The Hunchback of Notre Dame* in 1923. His gruesome makeup design for *The Phantom of the Opera* in 1925 set a standard for all horror films to follow; today, the horror genre has inspired some of the most inventive and memorable makeup effects in film history.

The Job

Some of makeup artist Vincent Guastini's recent creations involved turning Alanis Morissette into God and Matt Damon and Ben Affleck into angels. These effects for the film *Dogma* hearken back to the earliest examples of theatrical makeup, back to the Middle Ages when makeup effects were used to represent God, angels, and devils. But Guastini isn't relying on the simple symbolic face painting of the past; this production demanded that he design complicated animatronic wings, detailed rubber masks, and radio-controlled mechanical creatures. With a crew of some of the top makeup artists in the business, Guastini creates effects using rubber, plastic, fiberglass, latex paints, radio-control units from model airplanes, and steel cables. "As well as," Guastini says, "the old standby of a makeup kit filled with grease paints, makeup, rubber glues, brushes, and powders."

From a seven-foot tall alien for the film *Metamorphosis: The Alien Factor* to the animatronic killer doll Chucky in *Child's Play III*, Guastini has created some very bizarre and disturbing effects. "Movies like *Star Wars* and horror movies left an impact on me as a kid," Guastini says, citing his inspirations. He is also called upon to create less extreme transformations with makeup; his production company worked on *The Last of the Mohicans*, which involved applying wounds and prosthetics to hundreds of actors and extras.

Not every project involves prosthetics and special effects. Makeup artists also apply "clean" makeup, which is a technique of applying foundations and powders to keep actors and models looking natural under the harsh lighting of stage and film productions. Makeup artists accent, or downplay, an actor's natural features. They conceal an actor's scars, skin blemishes, tattoos, and wrinkles, as well as apply these things when needed for the character. Having read the script and met with the director and technicians, makeup artists take into consideration many factors: the age of the characters, the setting of the production, the time period, lighting effects, and other details that determine how an actor should appear. Historical productions require a great deal of research to learn about the hair and clothing styles of the time. Makeup artists also style hair, apply wigs, bald caps, beards, and sideburns, and temporarily color hair. In many states, however, makeup artists are limited in the hair services they can perform; some productions bring in locally licensed cosmetologists for hair cutting, dye jobs, and perms.

After much preparation, the makeup artist becomes an important backstage presence during a production. Throughout the making of a film, makeup artists arrive early for work every day. On the set of *Dogma*, preparing an actor's makeup took from four to six hours. "We were always the first to arrive and the last to leave the set," Guastini says of his crew of artists. Makeup artists are required to maintain the actors' proper makeup throughout filming and to help the actors remove the makeup at the end of the day. With the aid of fluorescent lighting, makeup artists apply the makeup, and they keep their eyes on the monitors during filming to make sure the makeup looks right. Guastini's production crew is also responsible for the mechanical creatures they create. "We must do constant repairs and upkeep on any mechanical creatures, making sure they're in working order," Guastini says.

Most makeup artists for film are in business for themselves, contracting work from studios, production companies, and special effects houses on a freelance basis. They may supplement their film work with projects for TV, video, commercials, industrial films, and photo shoots for professional photographers. Makeup artists for theater may also work freelance or be employed full-time by a theater or theater troupe. Makeup artists for theater find work with regional theaters, touring shows, and recreational parks.

Requirements

HIGH SCHOOL
Does becoming a makeup artist sound interesting to you? If so, there are a number of classes you can take in high school to help prepare you for this profession. Take all the art classes you can, including art history if this is offered at your school. Photography courses will help you understand the use of light and shadow. Courses in illustration, painting, and

drawing will help you to develop the skills you'll need for illustrating proposed makeup effects. Learning about sculpting is important, as creating special makeup effects with rubber, prosthetics, and glue is often much like sculpting from clay. Other helpful classes for you to take are anatomy and chemistry. Anatomy will give you an understanding of the human body, and chemistry will give you insight into the products you will be using. If your school offers drama classes, be sure to take these. In drama class you will gain an understanding of all the different elements—such as scripts, actors, and location—needed for a production. Computer classes will give you exposure to this technology, which you may use in the future to design projects. Try experimenting with makeup and special effects on your own. Take photographs of your efforts in order to build a portfolio of your work. Finally, because this work is typically done on a freelance basis and you will need to manage your business accounts, it will be helpful for you to take math, business, and accounting classes.

POSTSECONDARY TRAINING
There are a number of postsecondary educational routes you can take to become a makeup artist. If you have experience and a portfolio to show off your work, you may be able to enter the business right out of high school. This route is not always advisable, however, because your chances for establishing a successful freelance career without further training are slim. You must be very ambitious, enthusiastic, and capable of seeking out successful mentors willing to teach you the ropes. This can mean a lot of time working for free or for very little pay.

Another route you can take is to get specific training for makeup artistry through vocational schools. One advantage of this route is that after graduating from the program, you will be able to use the school's placement office, instructors, and other graduates as possible networking sources for jobs. Probably the most highly respected schools for makeup artists in film are the Joe Blasco schools, which have several locations across the country. Topics you might study at a Joe Blasco school include beauty makeup, old age makeup, bald cap usage, hairwork, and monster makeup. Some people in the business have cosmetology degrees, also offered by vocational schools. A cosmetology course of study, however, is not typically geared toward preparing you for makeup artistry work in the entertainment industry.

A third route you can take is to get a broad-based college or university education that results in either a bachelor's or master's degree. Popular majors for makeup artists include theater, art history, film history, photography, and fashion merchandising. In addition to makeup courses, it is important to take classes in painting, illustration, computer design, and animation. A master of fine arts degree in theater or filmmaking will allow you to gain hands-on experience in production as well as work with a faculty of practicing artists.

OTHER REQUIREMENTS

Patience and the ability to get along well with people are important for a makeup artist—throughout a film production, the actors will spend many hours in the makeup chair. Though many actors will be easy to work with, you may have to put up with much irritability, as well as overwhelming egos. Producers and directors can also be difficult to work with. And, as you gain more experience, you may have more knowledge about filmmaking than some of the producers of the projects. This may put you in frustrating situations, and you may see time wasted on costly mistakes.

Attention to detail is important; you must be quick to spot any makeup problems before they are filmed. Such responsibilities can be stressful—a whole production team will be relying on you to properly apply makeup that will look good on film. If your work isn't up to par, the whole production will suffer. Work as a makeup artist requires as much creativity and ingenuity as any other filmmaking task. The directors and actors rely on the makeup artists to come up with interesting makeup effects and solutions to filming problems. "It's important to be original in your work," Vincent Guastini advises. Guastini is also an example of the importance of ambition and dedication—within five years of graduating high school, he began work on his first motion picture. A year after that first assignment, he had developed a list of clients and put together a team of special effects artists. Because of the tough, competitive nature of the entertainment industry, makeup artists must be persistent and enthusiastic in their pursuit of work.

As a makeup artist, you may want to consider joining a union. The International Alliance of Theatrical Stage Employees (IATSE) represents workers in theater, film, and television production. Hair stylists, makeup artists, engineers, art directors, and set designers are some of the professionals who belong to the 500 local unions affiliated with IATSE. Union membership is not required of most makeup artists for film and theater, but it can help individuals negotiate better wages, benefits, and working conditions. Theaters in larger cities may require union membership of makeup artists, while smaller, regional theaters across the country are less likely to require membership.

Exploring

High school drama departments or local community theaters can provide you with great opportunities to explore the makeup artist's work. Volunteer to assist with makeup during a stage production and you will learn about the materials and tools of a makeup kit as well as see your work under stage lights. A high school video production team or film department may also offer you opportunities for makeup experience.

Most states have their own film commissions that are responsible for promoting film locales and inviting film productions to the local area. These film commissions generally need volunteers and may have internships for students. By working for a film commission, you will learn about productions coming to your state and may have the chance to work on the productions. Film industry publications such as *Variety* (http://www.variety.com) and *Entertainment Employment Journal* (http://www.eej.com) can alert you to internship opportunities.

The summer is a great time for students interested in stage production to gain firsthand experience. There are probably local productions in your area, but summer theaters often promote positions nationally. The Theatre Communications Group publishes a directory of nonprofit professional theaters across the country. Their bimonthly publication, *ArtSEARCH*, provides information on summer theater positions and internships.

Finally, explore this career by reading other publications for the field. For example, check out *Make-Up Artist Magazine* (http://www.makeup mag.com), a bimonthly publication with profiles of makeup artists for film as well as how-to columns and product information.

Employers

Although makeup artists work in a wide variety of circumstances, from theater to television to movies, they usually are self-employed, contracting individual jobs. Theater troupes, touring shows, and amusement parks may hire makeup artists on to their staffs, but in the film industry, makeup artists work on a freelance basis. Large cities and metropolitan areas will provide the majority of jobs for makeup artists, particularly those cities associated with thriving theaters, movie or television studios, fashion photography, and modeling/talent agencies. Although there may be some jobs in smaller towns, they probably will be mostly along the lines of industrial films, corporate videos, and photographic shoots—not very promising for those who wish to make a living in this line of work. Those who aspire to work exclusively as makeup artists gravitate toward the big cities.

Starting Out

You should keep a photographic record of all the work you do for theater and film productions, including photos of any drawings or sculptures you've done for art classes. It's important to have a portfolio to send along with your resume to effects shops, makeup departments, and producers. "Be prepared to work for free or for little money at the start," Vincent Guastini advises, "just to hook up with the right person who will hire you the next time out." To build up a portfolio of photographs, experiment in art classes and at home with makeup and special effects and photograph the results. Check with local TV studios about work in their makeup departments. Locally produced newscasts, children's programming, documentaries, and commercials offer opportunities for makeup artists. Commercials are often quick productions (between one and three days) with small casts, and they pay well. Department stores hire makeup artists to demonstrate and sell cosmetic products in department stores, which may be a starting position for those who want to earn a salary while getting on-the-job training and practice.

Because of the freelance nature of the business, you'll be going from project to project. This requires you to constantly seek out work. Read industry trade magazines such as *Variety*, and don't be shy about submitting your portfolio to producers and studios. Self-promotion will be an important part of your success as a makeup artist.

Advancement

Many makeup artists start as assistants or volunteers on a production, making contacts and connections. They eventually take on projects for which they are in charge of makeup departments and designing makeup effects. They may also establish their own production companies and make their own films or stage their own plays. "I would love to direct someday," Guastini says about his future, "or produce a film, but the project first time out should be a really solid, visually exciting film that incorporates my current talents."

Successful, experienced makeup artists can pick and choose their projects and work as much as they like. In the early years, makeup artists must frequently take on a variety of different projects just for the money; however, as they become established in the field and develop a solid reputation, they can concentrate on projects specific to their interests.

Earnings

Makeup artists usually contract with a production, negotiating a daily rate. This rate can vary greatly from project to project, depending on the budget of the production, the prestige of the project, and other factors. Even well-established makeup artists occasionally forgo payment to work on the low-budget independent productions of filmmakers they respect.

Independent contractors don't draw steady, yearly salaries. This means they may work long hours for several weeks, then, upon completion of a production, go without work for several weeks. Unless makeup artists are part of the union, they may be without benefits, having to provide all their own health insurance. An experienced makeup artist can make around $300 a day on a film with a sizable budget; some of the top makeup artists in the business command around $1,000 a day. Theatrical makeup artists can make comparable daily wages on Broadway, or in a theater in a large city; some small theaters, however, may pay only around $50 a day.

Because of such variables as the unsteady nature of the work, the makeup artist's experience, and even where he or she works, the yearly incomes for these individuals vary widely. Some makeup artists may show yearly earnings little higher than those resulting from the minimum wage. Others may have annual income in the hundreds of thousands of dollars.

Work Environment

Long hours, deadlines, and tight budgets can result in high stress on a movie set. Because makeup artists move from production to production, they work with different groups of people all the time and in different locales and settings. Although this allows makeup artists the opportunity to travel, it may also make a makeup artist feel displaced. While working on a production, makeup artists may have to forgo a social life, working long hours to design effects and prepare the actors for filming. The workdays may be twice as long as in the average workplace, and those work hours may be a stressful combination of working hurriedly and then waiting.

For those passionate about the work, however, any uncomfortable or frustrating conditions are easily overlooked. "I like creating something from nothing and seeing it alive and moving," Vincent Guastini says in regard to the creatures he has constructed for special effects. He also appreciates the travel and variety. "I like the people I meet," he says, "and the job is always different no matter the project or effect."

When working for the theater, the conditions are generally more controlled. With the exception of outdoor productions, theatrical makeup artists work in the dressing and makeup rooms of theaters and concert halls. The work can be very stressful, however, as the actors hurry to prepare for live productions.

Outlook

Makeup artists will find their opportunities increasing in the film and television industries. Digital TV has made it possible for hundreds of cable channels to be piped into our homes. The original programming needed to fill the schedules of these new channels results in jobs for makeup artists. Makeup effects artists will find challenging and well-paying work as the film industry pushes the envelope on special effects. These makeup artists may be using computers more and more, as digital design becomes an important tool in creating film effects.

Funding for theaters, some of which comes from the National Endowment for the Arts, is always limited and may be reduced during economic downturns or when productions are unpopular. During these times many theaters may be unable to hire the cast and crew needed for new productions. There has been a revived interest in Broadway, however, due to highly successful musicals such as *Rent* and *The Lion King*. This interest could result in better business for traveling productions as well as regional theaters across the country.

There will be a continuing need for makeup artists in still photography to prepare models for catalog and magazine shoots.

For More Information

For information on IATSE, a union representing over 100,000 members in entertainment and related fields in the United States and Canada, contact:

INTERNATIONAL ALLIANCE OF THEATRICAL STAGE EMPLOYEES (IATSE)
1430 Broadway, 20th Floor
New York, NY 10018
Tel: 212-730-1770
Web: http://www.iatse.lm.com

For information about how to order a copy of or subscription to Make-Up Artist Magazine, *contact:*

MAKE-UP ARTIST MAGAZINE
PO Box 4316
Sunland, CA 91041-4316
Tel: 818-504-6770
Web: http://www.makeupmag.com

For information about theater jobs and a sample copy of ArtSEARCH, *contact:*

THEATRE COMMUNICATIONS GROUP
355 Lexington Avenue
New York, NY 10017
Tel: 212-697-5230
Email: tcg@tcg.org
Web: http://www.tcg.org

For information about the Joe Blasco schools and careers in makeup artistry, check out the Web site:

JOE BLASCO MAKEUP TRAINING AND COSMETICS
Web: http://www.makeupacademy.com

Massage Therapists

Overview

Massage therapy is a broad term referring to a number of health-related practices, including Swedish massage, sports massage, Rolfing, Shiatsu and acupressure, trigger point therapy, and reflexology. Although the techniques vary, most *massage therapists* (or *massotherapists*) press and rub the skin and muscles. Relaxed muscles, improved blood circulation and joint mobility, reduced stress and anxiety, and decreased recovery time for sprains and injured muscles are just a few of the potential benefits of massage therapy. Massage therapists are sometimes called *bodyworkers*. The titles *masseur* and *masseuse,* once common, are now rare among those who use massage for therapy and rehabilitation. There are 34,000 massage therapists employed in the United States.

History

Getting a massage used to be considered a luxury reserved only for the very wealthy, or an occasional splurge for the less affluent. Some people thought massage to be a cover for illicit activities such as prostitution. With increased regulation of certification and a trend toward ergonomics in the home and workplace, however, massage therapy is recognized as an important tool in both alternative and preventive health care. Regular massage can help alleviate physical ailments faced by people today: physical stress brought on by an increase in sedentary lifestyle, aches and pains from hours spent in front of the computer, as well as injuries of the weekend warrior trying to make up for five days of inactivity.

The Job

Massage therapists work to produce physical, mental, and emotional benefits through the manipulation of the body's soft tissue. Auxiliary methods, such as the movement of joints and the application of dry and steam heat, are also used. Among the potential physical benefits are the release of muscle tension and stiffness, reduced blood pressure, better blood circulation, a shorter healing time for sprains and pulled muscles, increased flexibility and greater range of motion in the joints, and reduced swelling from edema (excess fluid buildup in body tissue). Massage may also improve posture, strengthen the immune system, and reduce the formation of scar tissue.

Mental and emotional benefits include a relaxed state of mind, reduced stress and anxiety, clearer thinking, and a general sense of well-being. Physical, mental, and emotional health are all interconnected: being physically fit and healthy can improve emotional health, just as a positive mental attitude can bolster the immune system to help the body fight off infection. A release of muscle tension also leads to reduced stress and anxiety, and physical manipulation of sore muscles can help speed the healing process.

There are many different approaches a massage therapist may take. Among the most popular are Swedish massage, sports massage, Rolfing, Shiatsu and acupressure, and trigger point therapy.

In Swedish massage the traditional techniques are effleurage, petrissage, friction, and tapotement. Effleurage (stroking), the use of light and hard rhythmic stroking movements, is used to relax muscles and improve blood circulation. It is often performed at the beginning and end of a massage session. Petrissage (kneading) is the rhythmic squeezing, pressing, and lifting of a muscle. For friction, the fingers, thumb, or palm or heel of the hand are pressed into the skin with a small circular movement. The massage therapist's fingers are sometimes pressed deeply into a joint. Tapotement (tapping), in which the hands strike the skin in rapid succession, is used to improve blood circulation. During the session the client, covered with sheets, lies undressed on a padded table. Oil or lotion is used to smooth the skin. Some massage therapists use aromatherapy, adding fragrant essences to the oil to relax the client and stimulate circulation. Swedish massage may employ a number of auxiliary techniques, including the use of rollers, belts, and vibrators; steam and dry heat; ultraviolet and infrared light; and saunas, whirlpools, steam baths, and packs of hot water or ice.

Sports massage is essentially Swedish massage used in the context of athletics. A light massage generally is given before an event or game to loosen and warm the muscles. This reduces the chance of injury and may improve performance. After the event the athlete is massaged more deeply to alleviate pain, reduce stiffness, and promote healing.

Rolfing, developed by American Ida Rolf, involves deep, sometimes painful massage. Intense pressure is applied to various parts of the body. Rolfing practitioners believe that emotional disturbances, physical pain, and other problems can occur when the body is out of alignment—for example, as a result of poor posture. This method takes 10 sessions to complete.

Like the ancient Oriental science of acupuncture, Shiatsu and acupressure are based on the concept of meridians, or invisible channels of flowing energy in the body. The massage therapist presses down on particular points along these channels to release blocked energy and untie knots of muscle tension. For this approach the patient wears loosely fitted clothes, lies on the floor or on a futon, and is not given oil or lotion for the skin.

Trigger point therapy, a neuromuscular technique, focuses in on a painful area, or trigger point, in a muscle. A trigger point might be associated with a problem in another part of the body. Using the fingers or an instrument, such as a rounded piece of wood, concentrated pressure is placed on the irritated area in order to "deactivate" the trigger point.

All of these methods of massage can be altered and intermingled depending on the client's needs. Massage therapists can be proficient in one or many of the methods, and they usually tailor a session to the individual.

Requirements

HIGH SCHOOL

Since massage therapists need to know more than just technical skills, many practitioners use the basic knowledge learned in high school as a foundation to build a solid career in the field. During your high school years, you should take fundamental science courses, such as chemistry, anatomy, and biology. These classes will give you a basic understanding of the human body and prepare you for the health and anatomy classes you will take while completing your postsecondary education. English, psychology, and other classes relating to communications and human development will also be useful, as the successful massage therapist is able to express his or her ideas with clients as well as understand the clients' reactions to the therapy. If you think you might wish to run your own massage therapy business someday, computer and business courses are essential. Finally, don't neglect your own physical well-being. Take physical education and health courses to strengthen your body and your understanding of your own conditioning.

POSTSECONDARY TRAINING

The best way to become a successful massage therapist is to attend an accredited massage therapy school after you have finished high school. In the United States, there are more than 65 schools accredited or approved by the Commission on Massage Therapy Accreditation (COMTA), a major accrediting agency for massage therapy programs and an affiliate of the American Massage Therapy Association (AMTA). COMTA-accredited and -approved schools must provide at least 500 hours of classroom instruction (this minimum is set to increase to 600 hours by March 1, 2003). Studies should include such courses as anatomy, physiology, theory and practice of massage therapy, and ethics. In addition, students should receive supervised hands-on experience. Most programs offer students the opportunity to participate at clinics, such as those providing massage services at hospices, hospitals, and shelters, or at school clinics that are open to the general public.

Massage therapy training programs typically take about a year to complete. Students can specialize in particular disciplines, such as infant massage or rehabilitative massage. Basic first aid and cardiopulmonary resuscitation (CPR) must also be learned. When choosing a school, you should pay close attention to the philosophy and curricula of the program, since a wide range of program options exist. Also, keep in mind that licensure requirements for massage therapists vary by state. For example, some state medical boards require students to have completed more than 500 hours of instruction before they can be recognized as massage therapists. Part of your process for choosing a school, therefore, should include making sure that the school's curriculum will allow you to meet your state's requirements.

CERTIFICATION OR LICENSING

Currently more than 25 states and the District of Columbia regulate the practice of massage therapy, requiring licensure, certification, or registration. Because requirements for licensing, certification, registration, and even local ordinances vary, however, you will need to check with your state's department of regulatory agencies to get specifics for your area. Typically, requirements include completing an accredited program and passing a written test and a demonstration of massage therapy techniques. Since 1992, the National Certification Board for Therapeutic Massage and Bodywork has offered a certification exam covering massage theory and practice, human anatomy, physiology, kinesiology, business practices, and associated techniques and methods. Those who pass the exam may use the designation Nationally Certified in Therapeutic Massage and Bodywork (NCTMB). Legislation is currently being considered to regulate certification across the country. Certification is highly recommended, since it demonstrates a therapist's high level of education and achievement. Certification may also make a therapist a more desirable candidate for job openings.

OTHER REQUIREMENTS

Physical requirements of massage therapists generally include the ability to use their hands and other tools to rub or press on the client's body. Manual dexterity is usually required to administer the treatments, as is the ability to stand for at least an hour at a time. Special modifications or accommodations can often be made for persons with different abilities.

It is important for a person interested in becoming a massage therapist to be nurturing and caring. Constance Bickford, a certified massage therapist in Chicago, thinks that it is necessary to be both flexible and creative: easily adaptable to the needs of the client, as well as able to use different techniques to help the client feel better. Listening well and responding to the client is vital, as is focusing all attention on the task at hand. A massage therapist needs to tune in to the person he or she is working on rather than zone out, thinking about the grocery list or what to cook for supper. An effective massage is a mindful one, where massage therapist and client work together toward improved health.

A massage therapist should also be trustworthy and sensitive. Someone receiving a massage may feel awkward lying naked in an office covered by a sheet, listening to music while a stranger kneads his or her muscles. A good massage therapist will make the client feel comfortable in what could potentially be perceived as a vulnerable situation.

People considering opening up their own businesses should be prepared for busy and slow times. In order to both serve their clients well and stay in business, they should be adequately staffed during rush seasons, and they must be financially able to withstand dry spells.

Exploring

The best way to become familiar with massage therapy is to get a massage. Look for a certified therapist in your area and make an appointment for a session. If you can afford it, consider going to several different therapists who offer different types of massage. Also, ask if you can set up an informational interview with one of the therapists. Explain that you are interested in pursuing this career, and come to the interview prepared to ask questions. What is this massage therapist's educational background? Why was he or she drawn to the job? What is the best part of this work? By talking to a massage therapist, you may also have the chance to develop a mentoring relationship with him or her.

A less costly approach is to find a book on massage instruction at a local public library or bookstore. Massage techniques can then be practiced at home. Books on self-massage are available. Many books discuss in detail the theoretical basis for the techniques. Videos that demonstrate massage techniques are available as well.

Consider volunteering at a hospice, nursing home, or shelter. This work will give you experience in caring for others and help you develop good listening skills. It is important for massage therapists to listen well and respond appropriately to their clients' needs. The massage therapist must make clients feel comfortable, and volunteer work can help foster the skills necessary to achieve this.

Employers

After graduating from an accredited school of massage therapy, there are a number of possibilities for employment. Doctors' offices, hospitals, clinics, health clubs, resorts, country clubs, cruise ships, community service organizations, and nursing homes, for example, all employ massage therapists. Some chiropractors have a massage therapist on staff to whom they can refer patients. A number of massage therapists run their own businesses. Most opportunities for work will be in larger, urban areas with population growth, although massage therapy is slowly spreading to more rural areas as well.

Starting Out

There are a number of resources you can use to locate a job. The AMTA offers job placement information to certified massage therapists who belong to the organization. Massage therapy schools have job placement offices. Newspapers often list jobs. Some graduates are able to enter the field as self-employed massage therapists, scheduling their own appointments and managing their own offices.

Networking is a valuable tool in maintaining a successful massage therapy enterprise. Many massage therapists get clients through referrals and often rely on word of mouth to build a solid customer base. Beginning massage therapists might wish to consult businesses about arranging onsite massage sessions for their employees.

Health fairs are also good places to distribute information about massage therapy practices and learn about other services in the industry. Often, organizers of large sporting events will employ massage therapists to give massages to athletes at the finish line. These events may include marathons and runs or bike rides done to raise money for charitable organizations.

Advancement

For self-employed massage therapists, advancement is measured by reputation, the ability to draw clients, and the fees charged for services. Health clubs, country clubs, and other institutions have supervisory positions for massage therapists. In a community service organization, massage therapists may be promoted to the position of health service director. Licensed massage therapists often become instructors or advisors at schools for massage therapy. They may also make themselves available to advise individuals or companies on the short- and long-term benefits of massage therapy, and how massage therapy can be introduced into professional work environments.

Earnings

The earnings of massage therapists vary greatly with the level of experience and location of practice. Therapists in New York and California, for example, typically charge higher rates than those in other parts of the country. Some entry-level massage therapists earn as little as minimum wage (ending up with a yearly income of around $11,000), but with experience, a massage therapist can charge from $10 to $70 for a one-hour session.

The *Occupational Outlook Quarterly (OOQ)* reported in 2000 that massage therapists who worked at least six hours a week had median yearly incomes ranging from $20,000 to $29,000. The *OOQ* also reported that massage therapists earned an average of $48 per hour. An article in *USA Today* profiling the career of massage therapist reports hourly earnings ranging from $40 to $110 in 2000. Those with earnings at the high end typically worked in higher-paying geographic areas (such as large cities), had years of experience, and had built up a large clientele. For therapists who worked in spas, salons, resorts, and gyms, *USA Today* notes earnings of $10 to $30 per hour, plus tips (which can add thousands of dollars to annual incomes). For massage therapists working full-time, the article estimated yearly earnings of approximately $35,000 to $40,000. Well-established therapists who manage to schedule an average of 20 clients a week for one-hour sessions can earn more than $40,000 annually. According to salary information from Health Care Job Store, an employment service for those in the health care industry, the average annual salary for massage therapists in the United States was approximately $30,380 in 2001.

More than two-thirds of all massage therapists are self-employed, and self-employed therapists are not paid for the time spent on bookkeeping, maintaining their offices, waiting for customers to arrive, and looking for new clients. In addition, they must pay a self-employment tax and provide their own benefits. With membership in some national organizations, self-employed massage therapists may be eligible for group life, health, liability, and renter's insurance through the organization's insurance agency.

Massage therapists employed by a health club usually get free or discounted memberships to the club. Those who work for resorts or on cruise ships can get free or discounted travel and accommodations, in addition to full access to the club's facilities when not on duty. Massage therapists employed by a sports team often get to attend the team's sporting events.

Work Environment

Massage therapists work in clean, comfortable settings. Because a relaxed environment is essential, the massage room may be dim, and soft music, scents, and oils are often used. Since massage therapists may see a number of people per day, it is important to maintain a hygienic working area. This involves changing sheets on the massage table after each client, as well as cleaning and sterilizing any implements used and washing hands frequently.

Massage therapists employed by businesses may use a portable massage chair—that is, a padded chair that leaves the client in a forward-leaning position ideal for massage of the back and neck. Some massage therapists work out of their homes or travel to the homes of their clients.

The workweek of a massage therapist is typically 35 to 40 hours, which may include evenings and weekends. On average, 20 hours or less per week are spent with clients, and the other hours are spent making appointments and taking care of other business-related details.

Since the physical work is sometimes demanding, massage therapists need to take measures to prevent repetitive stress disorders, such as carpal tunnel syndrome. Also, for their own personal safety, massage therapists who work out of their homes or have odd office hours need to be particularly careful about scheduling appointments with unknown clients.

Outlook

The U.S. Bureau of Labor Statistics reports there are 34,000 massage therapists in the United States. However, the professional organization Associated Bodywork and Massage Professionals estimates the number of trained therapists to be more than 140,000. The industry predicts a strong employment outlook for massage therapists through the next several years. The growing acceptance of massage therapy as an important health care discipline has led to the creation of additional jobs for massage therapists in many sectors.

One certified massage therapist points to sports massage as one of the fastest growing specialties in the field. The increasing popularity of professional sports has given massage therapists new opportunities to work as key members of a team's staff. Their growing presence in sports has made massage therapy more visible to the public, spreading the awareness of the physical benefits of massage.

Another growing opportunity for massage therapists is in the corporate world. Many employers eager to hold on to good employees offer perks, such as workplace massages. As a result, many massage therapists are working as mobile business consultants.

For More Information

For information on massage therapy and education programs, contact:
AMERICAN MASSAGE THERAPY ASSOCIATION
820 Davis Street, Suite 100
Evanston, IL 60201-4444
Tel: 847-864-0123
Web: http://www.amtamassage.org

For information on careers in the field, state board requirements, and training programs, contact:
ASSOCIATED BODYWORK AND MASSAGE PROFESSIONALS
1271 Sugarbush Drive
Evergreen, CO 80439-9766
Tel: 800-458-2267
Email: expectmore@abmp.com
Web: http://www.abmp.com

For information on accreditation and programs, contact:
COMMISSION ON MASSAGE THERAPY ACCREDITATION
820 Davis Street, Suite 100
Evanston, IL 60201
Tel: 847-869-5039
Email: info@comta.org
Web: http://www.comta.org

For information about state certification and education requirements, contact:
NATIONAL CERTIFICATION BOARD FOR THERAPEUTIC MASSAGE AND BODYWORK
8201 Greensboro Drive, Suite 300
McLcan, VA 22102
Tel: 800-296-0664
Web: http://www.ncbtmb.com

Mortuary Cosmetologists

Overview

A *mortuary cosmetologist* is a licensed cosmetologist who performs a variety of cosmetic services to prepare a deceased person for funeral services. Sometimes called *desairologists,* mortuary cosmetologists are trained to use products to style or alter the hair, face, or nails to prepare a deceased person for viewing and/or burial. In doing so, mortuary cosmetologists may provide comfort to grieving family and friends by making their deceased loved one appear as they wish them to be remembered. Mortuary cosmetologists are primarily cosmetologists who provide this additional service when requested, although full-time careers can be made of mortuary cosmetology. Approximately 709,000 cosmetologists, hairdressers, and hairstylists work in the United States.

History

In all societies, human bodies are prepared in some fashion before they are laid to rest. Archaeologists have discovered that the practice of preparing the dead dates back to the earliest Homo sapiens groups. The Neanderthals stained their dead with red ocher, a possible indication of some belief in afterlife. Throughout history, preparation of the dead has varied across cultures, but most practices included washing the body, dressing it in special garments, and adorning it with ornaments, religious objects, or mementos. Most of these practices continue throughout the world today.

Contemporary anthropological studies interpret funeral customs as symbolic expressions of the values that prevail in a particular society. In the United States, presentation of the body so that it appears natural and comfortable for its last public appearance is a part of the ritual.

Mortuary cosmetology as a career choice is fairly new, according to Noella C. Papagno, a practicing mortuary cosmetologist and author. Cosmetic preparation of the deceased is not a service that has evolved only with the mortuary cosmetologist. Funeral directors and embalmers have traditionally provided these services. As part of their licensing requirements, these professionals must be able to perform all preparations necessary—including applying makeup and styling hair. In many cases, the standard flesh-tone makeup is all that is needed. Those who had simple hairstyles, especially men, may not require the specialized services of a cosmetologist.

Mortuary cosmetology as a specialty was really only recognized in the late 1970s and early 1980s. Thanks to the efforts of Papagno and other cosmetology professionals, the funeral and cosmetology industries have come to realize that there is no reason why people who were particular about their appearance in life shouldn't have the same service available to them in death.

Today more schools are offering classes on mortuary cosmetology; they were unheard of in cosmetology schools a few decades ago. Papagno has published a book, *Handbook of Desairology for Cosmetologists Servicing Funeral Homes* (Jj Publishing, 1996). In that book, Papagno coined the term desairology (from the words deceased and hair), and many in the field prefer it to mortuary cosmetology.

The Job

Making the deceased appear as they did in life—the way their families want them to be remembered—is no small task. Occasionally, mortuary cosmetologists are asked to perform cosmetic services on a person they knew, often a client. But more frequently, mortuary cosmetologists work from a photograph provided by the family. Each situation is different—the quality of the photograph, difficulty of the style requested, conditions of death such as illness or trauma, and chemicals used in preparation of the body can all make the mortuary cosmetologist's job easier or more difficult.

Sterilizing and embalming chemicals used by funeral home personnel add to the dehydration process that occurs on a body, making the hair very dry and brittle. Also, the hair of decedents who were on medication before their deaths can be very thin and fall out easily when the cosmetologist attempts to cut or style it. In addition to these factors, the simple fact that the person who is being styled is in a horizontal rather than vertical position can be a challenge to a beginning mortuary cosmetologist. Denice Lafferty, a mortuary cosmetologist for 14 years, recalls that learning to roll hair the opposite direction to get it to set right was one of her biggest early challenges.

Getting over her uneasiness around the deceased was another challenge, Lafferty says, but it was something she grew accustomed to quicker than she expected. Her first mortuary job was for an elderly client she had grown close to. She styled the woman's hair regularly and visited her in the hospital before she died.

"I was scared to death the first time I was asked, but you have to keep in mind that this is the last thing you can do for this person. They (or the family) have put their trust in you," Lafferty says.

Despite the seemingly gloomy nature of the work, Lafferty notes the job is not without its rewards. "It's something you can't be prepared for, working with the dead. But after a while it doesn't bother you when you see what a valuable service you are providing. I get cards, thank you's, personal phone calls, and it makes you feel good that you were able to do that for somebody," she says.

As with most health care and funeral professionals, the initial experience dealing with the deceased usually evokes uneasiness. However, as mortuary cosmetologists gain more experience, the knowledge of the comfort they may provide to a grieving family generally helps offset their own discomfort. Also with experience comes a natural focus on the task at hand. Most mortuary cosmetologists are too busy to dwell on morbid thoughts; rather, their focus is on doing their job well for the sake of the family and the memory of the deceased. In general, mortuary cosmetologists do not handle the deceased beyond the preparations they are asked to make to the hair, face, or nails.

Requests for desairology services for deceased men are infrequent. On occasion, mortuary cosmetologists may be requested for a deceased man, based on the family's request or a trauma or illness requiring camouflage makeup.

Because the pores open after death, a transparent pancake makeup is applied to all deceased—men and women alike—in preparation for viewing. This makeup is generally applied by funeral home personnel, not the mortuary cosmetologist.

Most jobs are paid on a commission basis. In many cases, the funeral home bills the deceased's family for all services provided, even if the funeral home didn't directly provide them—including cosmetology services—so the family has just one bill to worry about. This also is done because the Federal Trade Commission requires funeral homes to disclose their fees to consumers on a general price list. The list includes the category "Other Preparation of Body," which means any preparation made to make the body presentable, including dressing, placing in casket, hair cutting, styling, and makeup.

Mortuary cosmetologists find clients in many different ways. If a mortuary cosmetologist has a relationship with a funeral home, the funeral home director may recommend him or her to a client who inquires about such services. Other clients may hear about a mortuary cosmetologist from their own beauticians, who may not provide such services. Also, mortuary cosmetologists seeking clients may find that listing their services in the yellow pages under funeral services is helpful, as well as leaving their business cards with salons who don't have their own mortuary cosmetologist on staff. Mortuary cosmetologists often do other work, and common places of employment include salons, malls, department stores, cruise ships, nursing homes, beauty supply stores, and cosmetic counters.

Requirements

HIGH SCHOOL
People outside the field of cosmetology are often surprised at the diverse subjects that cosmetology students must learn. High school classes that are also part of a college preparatory curriculum will help you if you plan to pursue this career. Science classes, such as physics, chemistry, and biology, will give you a background that you will find valuable years down the road—both in cosmetology school, when you learn specifically how those disciplines apply to the trade, and as a practicing cosmetologist, when you will use your knowledge to solve problems independently. In addition to science classes, mathematics courses such as algebra and geometry will give you preparation in working with numbers and formulas. Again, these are skills you will use in your later career. Of course, classes such as English and speech will allow you to

practice communication skills that will be important when you deal with a wide variety of people, some of whom will be experiencing a range of emotions. Also, because there is the possibility that you will be dealing with grieving families and friends of the deceased, consider taking psychology courses that will give you a greater understanding of people's reaction to stress and grief. Finally, if you have the opportunity, take art classes that will give you a chance to work with design and color.

Several high schools in the United States offer cosmetology programs as part of their vocational curriculum. At one such school, South Garland High School in Texas, students study bacteriology, electricity, and geometry to help them prepare for this work. Any student planning to pursue a career in cosmetology should keep in mind that most cosmetology schools require a high school diploma or general equivalency diploma and set a minimum age of 16.

POSTSECONDARY TRAINING

Cosmetology schools, still popularly known as beauty schools, prepare students for different careers in cosmetology. Cosmetology school generally requires 1,000 to 1,500 hours of training, which generally can be completed in a year. Many schools have classes starting throughout the year. According to the National Accrediting Commission of Cosmetology Arts and Sciences (NACCAS), no schools currently offer specific program sequences for mortuary cosmetologists. Many schools offer classes on mortuary services as part of their cosmetology curriculum, but states don't require special licensing for mortuary cosmetologists beyond the standard cosmetology license. Cosmetology schools offer training that leads to licenses in cosmetology (the full range of beauty services, including hair, skin, and nails), esthetics (which is limited to skin care, facial hair removal, and makeup), or nail technology (which is limited to care for the nails and cuticles on the hands and feet). Students of cosmetology can expect their curriculum to include classes in hair cutting and styling, permanent waves, tinting, eyebrow arching, facials, corrective makeup, manicuring, and pedicuring. These classes generally have students practice their new skills on mannequins or observe demonstrations. As students advance in their skills, they often practice on each other. Theory classes may include state law, chemistry, salon business management, and sterilization and sanitation. There are cosmetology schools in every state. Currently NACCAS has accredited approximately 1,000 schools that serve more than 100,000 students.

As a rule, general cosmetology internships are part of postsecondary schooling, although they usually are not called internships. Students advance to hands-on training only after they have completed the classroom and theoretical courses. Many cosmetology schools operate their own salons and offer discounted cosmetology services to the public, provided by cosmetology students in a supervised setting. Students observe and perform a specific type and number of procedures on clients to fulfill requirements of the school and the state they wish to practice in. In addition to passing a written exam, most states require a minimum number of hours of training on live subjects. During school "in-salon training," cosmetologists can expect to work at least 100 hours per month. Situations vary, but many cosmetologists-in-training receive a percentage of the fee for their work. Instructors, in addition to supervising techniques, use this time to give hints on building clientele, such as handing out business cards and explaining other services to the client. This practical experience is vital to launching a successful cosmetology career.

CERTIFICATION OR LICENSING

All 50 states require cosmetologists to be licensed. A person must be licensed—as a cosmetologist, funeral director, or embalmer—to perform cosmetic services on the deceased. In many funeral homes, unless the family requests special services or a certain cosmetologist, funeral home personnel do the necessary cosmetic preparations. Most mortuary schools require a class on restorative art that includes basic hairstyling and makeup techniques. Restorative art also covers more difficult body preparation work for bodies that have suffered a trauma, such as makeup to camouflage bruises and scrapes or techniques to rebuild a nose.

Only those who have completed the recommended training are permitted to apply for a cosmetology license. Although requirements vary by state, each state requires an application, generally with a minimal fee, and passage of a written examination. The exam determines the applicant's knowledge of pertinent areas such as product chemistry, sanitary rules and regulations, sanitary procedures, chemical service procedures, knowledge of the anatomy of the skin, provisions and requirements of the state in which they wish to practice, and knowledge of labor and compensation laws.

OTHER REQUIREMENTS

Cosmetology can be a physically and mentally demanding occupation, and the same applies to mortuary cosmetology. Cosmetologists are on their feet much of the day, and their work is very "hands-on." Because of the hands-on aspect of the work, mortuary cosmetologists must overcome any fears they may have about working with the dead. Mortuary cosmetologists need to have physical endurance in the shoulders and arms and finger dexterity because much of the time is spent cutting, trimming, or styling hair. Although the mortuary cosmetologist will not be expected to do strenuous physical work, carpal tunnel syndrome, which occurs when damage is done to nerves in the wrist because of repetitive hand motion, is a concern for any cosmetologist. Other helpful attributes for a mortuary cosmetologist to have include a sense of form and balance, the ability to imitate styles if a family has provided pictures of how they want the deceased to appear, and tact and understanding when dealing with families. The mortuary cosmetologist should also have a strong business sense. Since much of this work is done on a freelance basis, the cosmetologist will need to manage his or her finances.

Exploring

You can learn more about mortuary cosmetology by checking with local funeral homes, cosmetology schools, and salons. Most professionals are willing to take time to explain their work to students who show an interest. However, the extent to which they can show you the work they do may be limited. In order for an individual to observe cosmetic preparations on the deceased, the decedent's family must give permission. Many families may not be willing to do this. Families are especially reluctant to grant permission to a class, whether it is a high school vocational class or a cosmetology class, to be present for their loved one's preparation. You may have better results approaching a mortuary cosmetologist or funeral home director individually and stating your interest in the field.

Employers

Mortuary cosmetologists are rarely employed directly by funeral homes, particularly on a full-time basis. Since this area of cosmetology is relatively new, there generally is not yet a strong enough demand for these services to support full-time mortuary cosmetologists. Most are cosmetologists—either self-employed or employed by a salon—who provide mortuary services on a freelance basis. Many provide services to several funeral homes, especially in more rural areas, where there are fewer people who specialize in this work. In larger cities, one or two large funeral homes that see a high volume may provide enough business for a mortuary cosmetologist to make a part-time or even full-time income.

Starting Out

Few workers are directly involved in preparing the deceased for funerals: *directors, embalmers,* and *cosmetologists.* These professionals are the only people who can legally perform these services. Those interested in mortuary cosmetology should consider which aspects of the field appeal to them most in deciding whether to pursue funeral home or cosmetology training. Funeral home training takes longer than cosmetology training. Embalmers generally are required to complete two years of preprofessional college work—often resulting in an associate's degree. Funeral home directors are required to complete two years of college and then enroll in mortuary school for another year or two.

Those who have completed cosmetology training and are interested in this work should begin by aggressively marketing themselves to local funeral homes. Once the funeral homes know of a cosmetologist in the area who provides these services, they will be able to recommend the cosmetologist for work.

Advancement

A January 1998 article in the salon trade magazine *Techniques* discussed growth areas in the field of cosmetology, including mortuary cosmetology. The article noted that desairology may not hold the glamour of other cosmetology specialties, such as a stage or film artist, but it offers other attractions, such as the opportunity to perform humanitarian services. Mortuary cosmetologists who make funeral homes, salons, and the general public aware of the valuable service they provide can help their businesses grow. Mortuary cosmetologists who build a reputation for providing a valuable service can carve a niche for themselves in their area. Becoming a funeral home's or salon's designated desairologist can lead to steady work, which because of its specialized nature generally pays more than regular cosmetology services.

Earnings

The nature of the field of mortuary cosmetology, and indeed the field of cosmetology in general, is that earnings grow only as clientele increases. In any aspect of cosmetology, that means low earnings and hard work in the beginning. As cosmetologists develop client loyalty, their earnings will rise. In the mortuary cosmetologist's case, proving the value of one's services to a funeral home or a salon is the key to higher earnings. Mortuary cosmetologists charge more for their services to funeral homes than services in a salon. For example, a haircut and style may cost $10 to $20 in many areas. In the same area, a cut and style done on a visit to a funeral home will bring $30 to $40 because it is a specialized service. However, anyone planning to enter the field should remember it is a relatively new and highly specialized career, and demand is still somewhat limited. Mortuary cosmetology is not well known to the general public, and with the higher earnings comes the responsibility of marketing one's services to generate business.

Although specific information on earnings for mortuary cosmetologists is not available, the U.S. Department of Labor does have earning figures for the cosmetology field in general. Median annual earnings in 2000 for salaried hairdressers, hairstylists, and cosmetologists, including tips and commission, were $17,660. Salaries ranged from less than $12,280 to more than $33,220. According to the 1999 NACCAS Job Demand Survey, cosmetologists averaged hourly earnings of $18.50, which included tips. This hourly income translates into a yearly income of approximately $37,000 for full-time work. However, earnings are affected by factors such as number of clients, experience, and even location of the business.

Work Environment

Cosmetic procedures are generally done in a well-ventilated, sterile preparation room. Mortuary cosmetologists generally are not left alone with the deceased; a member of the funeral home staff will generally greet the cosmetologist and be present throughout the services if the cosmetologist desires. Mortuary cosmetologists are not expected to perform cosmetic procedures to a body on a table; rather, the body of the deceased is generally dressed and placed in the casket by the time the mortuary cosmetologist arrives to provide services.

Morticians, of course, work all hours. Their work depends basically on a person's time of death. Mortuary cosmetologists, on the other hand, may take an occasional call at an odd hour, but they generally perform their services at their earliest convenience. A cosmetologist usually has only a day's notice of services needed at a mortuary but can perform cosmetic services during day or evening hours, whatever is convenient.

Sanitation is of the utmost importance in funeral homes. Many of the extra steps funeral personnel take in preparation of the body and cleanup of the work area are for sanitary purposes, and mortuary cosmetologists must follow the same standards. Denice Lafferty, mortuary cosmetologist, uses basic equipment provided by the funeral home, such as a hair dryer, curling iron, and combs or brushes. This equipment is used only on the deceased and is thoroughly sterilized in a solution provided by the funeral home. On occasion she has to bring special equipment, such as a small curling iron or a bottle of temporary color. This equipment must be sterilized before she removes it from the funeral home. By the time mortuary cosmetology services are performed, the body has been embalmed, cleaned, and treated with chemical preservatives. Because of these chemicals and for sanitary purposes, mortuary cosmetologists always wear disposable gloves when they are performing cosmetic services.

Some widely held beliefs about bodies of the deceased may concern mortuary cosmetologists, who soon learn that such beliefs are unfounded, or at any rate, have little to do with their services. One commonly held belief is that the hair and nails continue to grow after death. Actually, the skin around the hair follicles and nail cuticles begins to shrink because of dehydration caused by death and the embalming process. Thus, the embedded portions of the hair and nails are exposed, giving the impression that they have grown. Another belief—that the deceased move—is not a myth. Rather, it is a rarity that some health care or morgue professionals have witnessed as the body is being handled. Morticians may also notice a rare movement, usually a small twitch, as the body is being prepared with chemicals—generally muscular responses as the chemicals used to preserve tissues are absorbed. The nature of the procedures mortuary cosmetologists perform means that they should not see such movement.

Outlook

The U.S. Department of Labor predicts the job growth for all cosmetologists to be about as fast as the average through 2010. The rate of growth for the specialty of mortuary cosmetology is dependent on two factors: how well those in the cosmetology industry market their services and the age of the population and number of deaths. According to statistics compiled by the National Funeral Directors Association, the death rate per thousand in the U.S. population is expected to increase significantly, from a projected rate of 8.82 deaths per thousand in 2000 to 10.24 deaths per thousand in 2020 and 13.67 per thousand in 2050. As the large baby boomer population ages, all careers that provide services to the elderly population are expected to experience steady growth.

For More Information

For statistics, information on individual schools, and career information, contact the following organizations:

NATIONAL ACCREDITING COMMISSION OF COSMETOLOGY
ARTS AND SCIENCES
4401 Ford Avenue, Suite 1300
Alexandria, VA 22302-1432
Tel: 703-600-7600
Web: http://www.naccas.org

NATIONAL FUNERAL DIRECTORS ASSOCIATION
13625 Bishop's Drive
Brookfield, WI 53005
Tel: 800-228-6332
Email: nfda@nfda.org
Web: http://www.nfda.org

Nail Technicians

Overview

Nail technicians clean, shape, and polish fingernails and toenails. They groom cuticles and apply cream to hands and arms (feet and calves in the case of pedicures). They apply a variety of artificial nails and provide ongoing maintenance. Many nail technicians are skilled in "nail art" and decorate clients' nails with stencils, glitter, and ornaments. Nail technicians may also call themselves *manicurists, pedicurists, nail sculpturists*, or *nail artists*. There are approximately 40,000 nail technicians working in the United States.

History

The word *manicure* comes from the Latin *manus* (hand) and *cura* (care). In ancient times, dramatically long and decorated fingernails were a mark of wealth and status, clearly distinguishing an aristocrat from a laborer. Historical artifacts reveal that the practice of caring for and decorating the fingernails dates back thousands of years. The excavation of one Assyrian tomb uncovered a 5,000-year-old cuticle stick. The ancient Egyptians used henna to stain their nails, and cosmetic kits have been discovered even in the tombs of Egyptian women, who took with them everything they might need in the next world.

Makeup remained in fashion throughout the Renaissance, although the Western ideal for fingernails was a natural look. Women took great pains to have soft, beautiful hands. They slept in gloves made from thin leather, lined with almond paste and oil from sperm whales. During this time, the Eastern habit of dyeing the nails and hands continued. Men and women alike were held to high standards for grooming of the hands during this time, as is evidenced in an 18th-century letter from the Earl of Chesterfield to his son: "Nothing looks more ordinary, vulgar, and illiberal, than dirty hands and ugly, uneven, ragged nails."

Predictably, the Victorian era frowned upon makeup. Decorative makeup was the mark of a loose woman, so the style for fingernails was au naturel. The end of the 19th century marked the advent of a change in this sentiment, when "nail powders" began to be advertised in Paris. Then, in 1907, liquid nail polish was introduced, the polish lightly tinted with rose dyes. For women who were wary of this new product, solid or powdered nail rouges were available. Nail kits containing files, orange sticks, cuticle implements, and so forth became popular in the first decade of the 20th century. The use of makeup was now becoming acceptable. *Vogue* asserted in 1920, "Even the most conservative and prejudiced people now concede that a woman exquisitely made up may yet be, in spite of seeming frivolity, a faithful wife and devoted mother."

Once the acceptability of makeup was established, a myriad of styles abounded in the 20th century. The year 1930 brought the invention of opaque nail polish as we know it today. Blood-red nails quickly became the rage, although the trendsetting Parisian women were soon sporting green, blue, white, and even black nails to match their clothing ensembles and jewels, sometimes even adding shocking decorative touches not unlike the handiwork of modern-day nail artists.

Also in 1930, *Harper's Bazaar* introduced the idea that fashionable women should match their nail polish and their lipstick. New colors began to flourish in the 1930s, including corals, pinks, and beiges. The 1940s brought yet more naturalistic colors in makeup. In America, Hollywood played a significant role in pushing makeup into the realm of the glamorous. Production of makeup slowed down during World War II as supplies became scarce. But the makeup frenzy exploded in the 1950s when the marketing geniuses at Revlon dictated that colors should change with the season, and women scrambled to get their hands on each new shade as it was introduced. It was also during the 1950s that a dentist in Philadelphia invented sculptured nails, which were quickly embraced and promoted by celebrities such as Cher and Tina Sinatra. Long, fashionable nails were now within the reach of all women.

Elizabeth Taylor's *Cleopatra* inspired the dramatic, dark-eyed look of the early 1960s, and the eyes continued to dominate the makeup scene into the 1970s, while lips and nails faded into the background. However, by 1972, wild nail colors were once again in full swing, and Revlon introduced a line called "Lady in the Dark," whose 24 shades included variations of green, purple, blue, and black. Of course, with the concurrent advent of the back-to-nature movement in the 1970s, not every women rushed out to buy the latest shade. A truly natural approach to self-care was also developing, which has been largely synthesized into the concepts and products of the last two decades.

Today, both decorative and natural makeup styles have an established place, and there are fingernail products and styles to suit everyone. While many nail products (including artificial nail kits) continue to be widely available at the retail level, more and more women—and men—are seeking out the services of professional nail technicians.

The Job

Nail technicians generally work at a manicurist table and chair or stool across from their clients. Their work implements include finger bowls, electric heaters, wet sanitizer containers, alcohol, nail sticks and files, cuticle instruments, emery boards and buffers, tweezers, nail polishes and removers, abrasives, creams and oils, and nail dryers.

Standard manicure procedure involves removing old polish, shaping nails, softening and trimming cuticles and applying cuticle cream, cleansing and drying hands and nails, applying polish and top coat, and applying hand lotion. As an extra service, lotion is often massaged into the wrists and arms as well as the hands. Technicians should always follow a sanitary cleanup procedure at their stations following each manicure, including sanitizing instruments and table, discarding used materials, and washing and drying their hands.

A man's manicure is a more conservative procedure than a woman's; the process is similar, but most men prefer to have a dry polish or to have their nails buffed.

Pedicuring has become a popular and important salon service, especially when fashion and weather dictate open-toed shoe styles. The procedure for a pedicure is much like that of a manicure, with the set-up involving a low stool for the technician and an ottoman for the client's feet.

Nail technicians also provide other services, including the application of artificial nails. A number of techniques are employed, depending on the individual client's preferences and nail characteristics. These include nail wrapping, nail sculpting, nail tipping, press-on nails, and nail dipping. Technicians also repair broken nails and do "fill-ins" on artificial nails as the real nails grow out.

Nail technicians must take care to use only new or sanitized instruments to prevent the spread of disease. The rapid growth of this industry has been accompanied by an increased awareness of the many ways in which viral, fungal, and bacterial infections can be spread. Many states have passed laws regarding the use of various instruments. Although nail technicians may be exposed to such contagious diseases as athlete's foot and ringworm, the use of gloves is not a practical solution due to the level of precision required in a nail technician's work. For this reason, nail technicians must be able to distinguish between skin or nail conditions that can be treated in the salon and disorders and diseases that require medical attention. In so doing, educated and honest nail technicians can contribute to the confidence, health, and well-being of their customers.

Requirements

HIGH SCHOOL

Many states require that nail technicians be high school graduates, although a few states require only an eighth- or tenth-grade education. If you are interested in becoming a nail technician, consider taking health and anatomy classes in high school. These classes will give you a basis for understanding skin and nail conditions. Since many nail technicians are self-employed, you may benefit from taking business classes that teach you how a successful business is run. Take art classes, such as painting, drawing, or sculpting, that will allow you to work with your hands and develop a sense of color and design. Finally, don't forget to take English or communication classes. These courses will help you hone your speaking and writing skills, skills that you will need when dealing with the public. Some high schools with vocational programs may offer cosmetology courses. Such courses may include the study of bacteriology, sanitation, and mathematics. These specialized courses can be helpful in preparing students for their future work. You will need to check with your high school about the availability of such a vocational program.

POSTSECONDARY TRAINING

Your next step on the road to becoming a nail technician is to attend a cosmetology or nail school. Some states have schools specifically for nail technician training; in other states, the course work must be completed within the context of a full cosmetology program. Nail technology courses generally require between 100 and 500 clock hours of training, but requirements can vary widely from state to state. Because of these variations, make sure the school you choose to attend will allow you to meet the educational requirements of the state in which you hope to work. When the required course work has been completed, the student must pass an examination that usually includes a written test and a practical examination to demonstrate mastery of required skills. A health certificate is sometimes required.

Course work in nail schools (or nail technician programs in cosmetology schools) reflects that students are expected to learn a great deal more than just manicuring; typical courses of study encompass a broad array of subjects. The course outline at Pivot Point International (in Illinois and Alabama) includes bacteriology, sanitation, and aseptic control procedures; diseases and disorders of the nail; anatomy (of the nails, hands, and feet); nail styling and artificial nail techniques; spa manicures and pedicures; aromatherapy; reflexology; state law; advertising and sales; and people skills. Course work also includes working on live models so that each student graduates with hands-on experience in each service studied.

CERTIFICATION OR LICENSING

Most states require nail technicians to be licensed. Usually a fee is charged to take the exam, and another fee is assessed before receiving the license. Exams usually include both written and practical tests. Many states now offer special nail technician licenses (sometimes called limited or specialty certificates), which require anywhere from 100 to 500 hours of schooling in a licensed cosmetology or nail school. In states where no limited certificates are offered, a student must complete cosmetology school (substantially more hours than required for a specialty), become licensed as a cosmetologist, and then specialize in nail technology. Some states offer special licenses for manicurist managers and nail technician instructors; these require substantially more hours of schooling than do nail technician licenses. Reciprocity agreements exist in some states that enable a nail technician to work in another state without being retested. Some states require that nail technicians be 16 or 18 years old in order to be licensed. You will need to find out the licensing requirements for the state in which you hope to work. Associations and state boards of health can often supply this information.

OTHER REQUIREMENTS

Nail technicians must have good vision and manual dexterity, as their work is very exacting in nature. Creativity and artistic talents are helpful, especially in those technicians who perform nail art, which can include painting designs and applying various decorative items to nails. A steady hand is important, and nail technicians should also have an eye for form and color.

Since nail technicians provide services to a wide variety of people, the personality and attitude of a nail technician to a large extent ultimately determine his or her success. While some clients are easy to please, others are demanding and even unreasonable; a nail technician who is able to satisfy even the most difficult customers will be positioned to develop a large, loyal following. Nail technicians who are punctual, courteous, respectful, and patient will enjoy a distinct competitive advantage over others in the industry who lack these qualities. Tact, professionalism, and competence are important. Knowledge and practice of proper sanitizing techniques should be clearly visible to clients. Naturally, hygiene and grooming are of paramount importance in this profession, and a nail technician's own hands and nails should be perfectly groomed; this is one's best form of advertisement and can help foster confidence in prospective and new clients.

A confident, outgoing personality can be a great boon to a nail technician's success. Customers may readily accept recommendations for additional nail services from a persuasive, knowledgeable, and competent nail technician who appears genuinely interested in the customer's interests. Nail technicians who can successfully sell their services will enjoy increased business.

Unlike most careers in the cosmetology field, nail technicians are not required to be on their feet all day. Nail technology is a good choice for those interested in the beauty industry who prefer to be able to work in a seated, comfortable position.

Exploring

If you are considering a career as a nail technician, a good avenue of exploration is to call a cosmetology or nail school and ask for an opportunity to tour the facilities, observe classes, and question instructors. Another enjoyable option is for you to make an appointment with a nail technician for a manicure or pedicure. By receiving one of these services yourself, you will have the opportunity to visit the place of business, take in the atmosphere, and experience the procedure. In addition, you'll have the opportunity to talk to someone who can answer your questions about this line of work. Explain that you are interested in becoming a nail technician, and you may find that you can develop a mentoring relationship with this professional technician. A part-time job in a beauty salon that offers nail services may also help you determine your interest in various aspects of the beauty industry. Part-time positions for nontechnicians in nail salons, though, may prove difficult to find.

Employers

As with cosmetologists and other personal appearance workers, approximately half of the nail technicians in the country are self-employed. They may rent a "booth" or chair at a salon; some may own their own nail salons. A growing number of nail technicians are employed by nail salons, which are rapidly increasing in number in many areas of the country. Beauty shops and department store salons also employ nail technicians, but most have only one or two on staff (very large salons have more). Since nail services represent one of the fastest-growing segments of the cosmetology industry, there is good potential for those wishing to open their own businesses in the nail industry.

Starting Out

In most states, graduating from an accredited cosmetology or nail school that meets the state's requirements for licensing is the vehicle for entry into this field. Nearly all cosmetology schools assist graduates with the process of finding employment. Want ads and personal visits to salons and shops are also productive means of finding a job.

Cindy Singer, president of the Illinois Nail Technicians Association (Illinois offers a separate license for nail technicians), asserts that working in a beauty salon is a terrific way for a nail technician to start out. While she estimates that perhaps half of all nail technicians are self-employed (whether they own their own shops or rent a space), she says, "There is no better way to build a clientele than to start out in a busy beauty salon with an established customer base." If nail technicians provide top-quality services and establish relationships with their customers, they will find that most clients will gladly follow them should they go into business for themselves.

Advancement

Advancement in the nail technology industry most often takes the form of establishing a large, loyal clientele. Other opportunities include owning one's own nail salon. This can be a highly profitable endeavor if one has the proper business skills and savvy; the cost of materials and overhead can be relatively low, and, in addition to the earnings realized from services performed for their customers, the owners typically receive half of their operators' earnings.

Some technicians choose to advance by becoming nail instructors in cosmetology or nail schools or becoming inspectors for state cosmetology boards.

Nail technicians who constantly strive to increase their knowledge and proficiency in a wide array of nail services will have a competitive advantage and will be positioned to secure a large and varied clientele.

Earnings

Income for nail technicians can vary widely, depending on the skill, experience, and clientele of the nail technician, the type and location of the shop or salon, the tipping habits of the clientele, and the area of the country. The U.S. Department of Labor reports the median annual income for nail technicians was $15,440 in 2000. (This income includes tips.) Salary.com, a provider of compensation information, reports that nationwide manicurists had yearly earnings ranging from approximately $14,470 to $17,590 in March of 2002. Those working in large metropolitian areas may have slightly higher earnings, but the cost of living is also higher there. According to findings by *NAILS Magazine*, which surveyed professionals to come up with 2000-2001 statistics on the industry, nail technicians serviced on average about 36 clients per week and charged on average approximately $14 for a manicure. Given these figures, a technician who works 50 weeks a year (with two weeks off for vacation) would earn $25,200. *NAILS Magazine* also reports the cost of a booth rental averaged about $342 per month ($4,104 per year). Deducting this charge from the technician's earnings leaves the technician with a base income of approximately $21,095. Obviously, tips have not been figured into this income, and they may raise earnings by several thousand dollars per year.

The importance of the talents and personality of the nail technician cannot be underestimated when evaluating potential earnings. Those who hold themselves to the highest levels of professionalism, express a genuine interest in clients' well-being, and provide the highest quality service quickly develop loyal clienteles, and these nail technicians will realize earnings that far exceed the averages.

Those technicians who work in beauty shops are less likely than those in nail salons to have appointments scheduled throughout the day; however, customers in beauty salons often pay more and tip better for these services. Also, there is less competition within the beauty shop setting, as the majority of beauty salons employ only one or two nail technicians.

Owning one's own nail salon can be very profitable, as the cost of equipment is relatively low. In addition to taking home one's own earnings from servicing clients, the owner also generally gets half of the income generated by the shop's other operators. Nail salons are a prime example of a small business with tremendous potential for success.

Except for those nail technicians who work in department stores or large salons, most do not enjoy much in the way of benefits; few nail technicians receive health and life insurance or paid vacations.

Work Environment

Nail technicians work indoors in bright, well-ventilated, comfortable environments. Unlike most careers in the cosmetology industry that require operators to be on their feet most of the day, nail technicians perform their work seated at a table.

Many nail technicians work five-day weeks including Saturdays, which are a high-volume business day in this industry. Working some evenings may be helpful in building one's clientele, as a large percentage of customers are working professionals. Nail technicians often enjoy some flexibility in their hours, and many enjoy successful part-time careers.

A large number of nail technicians are self-employed; they may rent a space in a beauty or nail salon. Often, nail technicians must provide their own supplies and tools. Nail technicians are exposed to a certain amount of chemicals and dust, but this is generally manageable in well-ventilated work surroundings. Those who work in full-service salons may be exposed to additional chemicals and odors.

Inherent in the nature of a nail technician's work is the constant company of others. A nail technician who is not a "people person" will find this line of work most challenging. But since most people who choose this career enjoy the company of others, they find the opportunity to talk with and get to know people to be one of the most satisfying and enjoyable aspects of their work.

Outlook

The nail business (a multibillion-dollar industry) has been growing rapidly for years. Nail salons and day spas offering nail services continue to crop up everywhere, and nail technicians represent the fastest-growing segment of the various specialized service providers in the beauty industry. According to the U.S. Department of Labor, employment for nail technicians should grow faster than the average through 2010. According to Cindy Singer of the Illinois Nail Technicians Institute, "There are more than 10,000 licensed nail technicians in Illinois alone, and approximately half of those work in the Chicagoland area. Large cities typically provide the bulk of job opportunities for nail technicians."

Once a mark of feminine status, nail services are now sought and enjoyed by a wide variety of people, both male and female. Helen Barkan, whose clients have dubbed her the "Nail Doctor," has been a nail technician and salon owner in the Deerbrook Mall in Deerfield, Illinois, for the past 24 years, and she has been doing nails for more years than she'll reveal. Barkan, whose straightforward services focus on helping clients grow strong, healthy nails (she doesn't do artificial nails), says, "Many of my clients have been coming to me for more than 20 years. I've always been willing to spend a little extra time and go the extra mile for my customers, and at one time I worked seven days a week. My clients are important to me, and they know that." Barkan has watched the industry change dramatically over the decades. Today, approximately one-third of Barkan's customers are men, and they come for manicures and pedicures alike. Clearly, there is a market for all kinds of nail services, from the most basic hand and nail care to the most involved procedures and outlandish styles.

For More Information

This organization of stylists, salon owners, nail technicians, and other professionals can provide industry and education information.
COSMETOLOGISTS CHICAGO
401 North Michigan Avenue
Chicago, IL 60611
Tel: 800-648-2505
Web: http://www.isnow.com

This magazine has information on the latest nail technologies, fashions, safety matters, and industry news.
NAILS MAGAZINE
21061 South Western Avenue
Torrance, CA 90501
Tel: 310-533-2400
Web: http://www.nailsmag.com

This organization accredits cosmetology schools nationally and can provide lists of licensed training schools.
NATIONAL ACCREDITING COMMISSION OF COSMETOLOGY ARTS AND SCIENCES
4401 Ford Avenue, Suite 1300
Alexandria, VA 22302-1342
Tel: 703-600-7600
Web: http://www.naccas.org

This Web site for beauty professionals has a state board listing of requirements for nail technicians.
BEAUTY TECH
Web: http://www.beautytech.com/nailtech

Salon Managers

Quick Facts

School Subjects
Art
Business
Health
Personal Skills
Communication/ideas
Leadership/management
Work Environment
Primarily indoors
Primarily one location
Minimum Education Level
Some postsecondary training
Salary Range
$16,700 to $37,000 to $71,000+
Certification or Licensing
Required for certain positions
Outlook
About as fast as the average

Overview

Salon managers may occupy positions in beauty salons, day spas, children's salons, nursing homes, and cruise lines. Their primary duties are to maintain a congenial rapport between clients and personnel, oversee the financial budget, manage inventory, and supervise employees. Salon managers must be personable, able to withstand the pressures of a rigorous day, and dressed for success, since their appearance can act as an advertisement for their salon. The manager is often responsible for hiring employees, policing their licenses, enforcing health and sanitary conditions, and maintaining accurate records. Each state stipulates its requirements for salons; in Washington, DC, the Cosmetology Act states "Every beauty salon shall have a manager, who shall have immediate charge and supervision over the operators practicing cosmetology."

History

The origin of beauty culture began in ancient times, when an attractive appearance was associated with physical well-being. Personal embellishments, such as kohl, a form of eye shadow, were used by the Egyptians, Sumerians, Hebrews, and Babylonians to adorn the dead, dress for political ceremony, and enhance individual grooming. The science of cosmetics continued beyond the fall of the Roman Empire, into the Renaissance, and finally to modern-day use. In 1914, cosmetic sales totaled $39.8 million, growing to $449.9 million in 1940; they climbed to $24.4 billion in 2000, and they are still expanding.

The origin of barbers also predates modern times. The Egyptian papyri (written papers) refer to barbers as conveyors of news and advice, and barbershops became a favorite meeting place. Early Christian monasteries bestowed on barbers the honor of shaving the hair of monks. In the Middle Ages, barbers treated medical illnesses, cauterizing wounds, treating abscesses, and extracting teeth. Barbers were referred to as "doctors of the short robe," while academically trained doctors were known as "doctors of the long robe." Barbers' knowledge of human anatomy and physiology combined with the cosmetic applications of creams, oils, and hair colorings to create the beauty culture of the modern day. The profession enhanced the creative and artistic talents of the cosmeticians, while it grew in tandem with the fashion world.

Hairstyling salons, which were once patronized only by the privileged class, have become commonplace. Today approximately 605,000 licensed cosmetologists work in the United States. As women continue to enter the business world and the pace of society quickens, time-efficient salons and salons/spas are in demand. New techniques in skin care, hair conditioning, and nail sculpture continue to add to the industry's popularity. Day spas have cropped up everywhere to offer total makeovers. Beauty-enhancing treatments, such as skin exfoliation, scalp massages, and pedicures with tension-busting acupressure, are familiar procedures in the relaxing environments of the beauty industry.

A good example of the growing salon industry is the Minneapolis-based cosmetics firm Aveda, now in business for over 20 years. The company has developed a million-dollar business, offering numerous products available in stores across the United States and other countries such as Canada, Germany, Indonesia, Iceland, and Italy. "Aveda is on the cutting edge when it comes to natural products," says David Vladyak, project manager with Kline and Company, a cosmetic market research firm. The Aveda spa in Wisconsin now incorporates aromatherapy into its pampering ritual; the company believes scented oils and creams are therapeutic, influencing moods and responses to stress.

Because cosmetologists have become absorbed in providing these many different services, they have little or no time to spend in management. This situation has created a need for efficient salon managers to free cosmetologists from routine business tasks.

The Job

A salon manager's responsibilities include business administration, public relations, and personnel management. Most crucial to success, however, is a wonderful personality and a positive mental outlook. "A good manager should always be upbeat and happy, and be a pleasant person at all times. It doesn't matter what is going on in your personal life," says Andrea Blackshaw, co-owner of The Scissor's Edge, a unisex hair salon in Winnetka, Illinois.

All salons should have financial budgets to allocate funds and good bookkeeping systems. Managers should maintain records of daily, weekly, and yearly expenses, as well as files on each patron. Managers must check to see if the dates of the operators' licenses are current. They should be familiar with insurance policies for fire, theft, and health, be on good terms with the salon's accountants and lawyers, and review the regulations established by the state board of cosmetology.

A large portion of the manager's job is based on the psychology of communication. The manager should be a good liaison between operators and clients and be readily available to handle complaints and adjustments with minimal fuss. The manager's role is to build good will; therefore, he or she should become acquainted with the different people who enter the salon. Verbal skills are important, and managers should instruct their receptionists on proper telephone etiquette; a receptionist with a pleasant tone and gentle mood invites the customer to return.

The salon's decor is often another managerial concern, and some managers function as design consultants as well. Arranging an attractive cosmetic display and keeping a spotless salon are also important considerations when creating a welcoming environment. Safety is a concern, too, so every salon manager must have access to a first-aid kit and a hospital telephone number, and he or she should be familiar with CPR.

Delaware, Maryland, Minnesota, North Dakota, Ohio, and South Dakota have separate laws for cosmeticians who are also managers; they are called manager-operators. Minnesota and Ohio require specific licenses for cosmetologists who only want to be a manicurist-manager. Manager-operators are often interim positions between doing cosmetology work and owning one's own business. Manager-operators must be licensed as cosmetologists within their state; they are paid a percentage of the salon's profits and, unlike managers who are not operators, they are allowed to style hair. They also have the advantage of prior experience and are already familiar with various aspects of the business.

Requirements

HIGH SCHOOL

Does working as a salon manager sound interesting to you? There are a number of courses you can take in high school to help prepare you for this career. Classes in health, anatomy, and chemistry will give you a science background that will be helpful in both your postsecondary education and your career when you will deal with sanitation issues, chemical products, and new procedures. Since managing finances will be in your future, take business, accounting, and mathematics classes. Computer classes that teach you how to work with spreadsheet programs will also be beneficial. Psychology classes may provide you with a basis for understanding people, which will be an asset when you work with a variety of customers and employees. Finally, take any studio art courses that you can. Painting, sculpting, or photography, for example, will give you the opportunity to develop your sense of color and design, important qualities for anyone working in the beauty industry.

Some high schools offer vocational programs in cosmetology, and some cosmetology schools allow high school students to begin their studies there as they also work to complete high school. In both of these specialized programs, students typically study such topics as sanitation procedures, sciences, mathematics, and even legal issues of the industry.

POSTSECONDARY TRAINING

Although a few salon managers may have only a business background, the majority of salon managers have risen to this position by first working as a cosmetologist, barber-stylist, or manager-operator. To become a cosmetologist or barber, plan on attending an accredited cosmetology or barber school. Full-time programs vary in length but generally last from 10 to 24 months. Work will include classroom study and hands-on experiences. You will study such topics as chemistry, hygiene, anatomy, and proper care of your tools and equipment. In addition, a good program will cover general business practices and legal issues. The National Accrediting Commission of Cosmetology Arts and Sciences (NACCAS) can provide you with a listing of accredited schools across the country. (The organization's contact information is given at the end of the article.) All states require barbers and cosmetologists to be licensed, but the requirements vary from state to state. It is important, therefore, that you find out what your state requires and make sure the program you are interested in will allow you to meet those requirements. Because the manager-operator position allows a professional to gain business and management experience, those who have worked in this position are often the best prepared to become full-time salon managers.

CERTIFICATION OR LICENSING

There is no certification or licensing for salon managers, per se, nor are there labor unions. However, a salon manager who is also a cosmetologist, barber, or manager-operator must be licensed. To receive a license you will need to pass a state exam, which is generally a written test but may also include a demonstration and an oral test. As noted above, requirements for licensing vary by state; therefore, you will need to determine the requirements for the state in which you hope to practice before you begin your education. Students who have passed their state test and applied for a license are issued temporary permits in most states. Temporary permits allow them to practice their profession while they wait to receive the actual license.

Even after a cosmetologist or barber has become licensed, his or her education must continue. Many states require cosmetologists and barbers to take a specified number of credit hours, called continuing-education units or CEUs, to keep their licenses current. Again, these requirements vary by state; state licensing boards will have complete information.

OTHER REQUIREMENTS

Hairstyles change from season to season. New techiques are continuously being developed for working with hair, nails, and skin. Customers' expectations of their salon experience also change with the times. Because the salon manager works in this dynamic environment, he or she should enjoy learning about new fashions and figuring out ways to provide new services to customers. The salon manager also needs to have an artistic sense or strong sense of personal style. The manager's looks are an advertisement for the salon; few customers will feel comfortable patronizing a salon where the manager has a bad dye job or ragged nails. And, naturally, the successful salon manager enjoys working with people. "Running a salon is like being a parent in the home," says Terri Ross, hair stylist and owner of J. Terri Ross in Glencoe, Illinois. "A manager solves problems, monitors clients, and takes care of the various personalities that enter. He should be open-minded, assertive, and stick to his guns in dealing with people. The best personality traits he can have are to be optimistic, even-tempered, hard-working, and go with the flow."

Exploring

Although you won't be able to experience the position of salon manager itself until you are qualified for this work, there are a number of steps you can take to explore this career. Contact a local cosmetology school and request a tour of the facilities. In addition, ask if you can sit in on a class or talk to the instructors and students. This will give you a sense of what the education is like and allow you to talk to others interested in the industry. Also, contact a local salon to arrange for an informational interview with either the salon manager or a cosmetologist. At an informational interview you can ask such questions as: What is the most enjoyable aspect of the job? What is the least enjoyable? What educational route did this professional take? What recommendations does he or she have for someone interested in the field? If the salon manager is receptive to the idea, you might be able to shadow him or her for a day to see what the typical business day is like. Also, read salon industry magazines, such as *Salon Business Strategies* (http://www.strategiespub.com) and *Salon Today* (http://www.salontoday.com), to find out what issues are important to those working in the field.

Consider gaining some business or management experience. Get a part-time or summer job in a salon or retail business in which you will have to work with customers and develop your people skills. Also, consider joining school clubs or organizations that allow you management roles on projects or give you the opportunity to work with the finances, perhaps by balancing the books or acting as treasurer.

Finally, try volunteering at a nursing home or hospital. In these environments you may be in a position to provide personal care services such as washing and styling a patient's hair. Any volunteer work in which you interact with people will also help you hone your communication skills.

Employers

Salon managers work in beauty salons, barbershops, children's salons, and nursing homes. They may also work at resorts, spas, and hotels, or for cruise lines. Generally there are more employment opportunities in large cities, which have a greater number of salons, day spas, and other such businesses.

Starting Out

Generally, a management position is not considered entry-level. Those hoping to become salon managers typically start out as cosmetologists or other stylists after graduating from cosmetology or barber school. These schools provide the opportunity for networking with others in the profession, which may lead to a job, and some may also have placement services for their graduates. Also, industry magazines, Web sites, and local newspapers frequently publish job openings. Trade shows and organization conferences may also provide the opportunity to network for jobs.

Advancement

Advancement to the position of salon manager comes through continuing education in the cosmetology field, networking with other professionals, and gaining business experience. Salon managers advance by moving to larger salons, where they oversee more employees and have a larger client base. Some managers work toward owning their own salons. Other avenues for advancement include moving into advertising or working in sales in the beauty industry. Success for any manager is largely based on self-motivation, continuous learning, and the ability to interact well with people.

Earnings

Although the U.S. Department of Labor does not provide specific salary information for salon managers, a salary range for these workers can be determined by reviewing earnings of others in the beauty and related industries. According to a 1999 survey by NACCAS, cosmetologists averaged hourly earnings of $18.50, including tips. This hourly income translates into a yearly income of approximately $37,000 for full-time work, and a cosmetologist working up to salon management may expect an income close to this figure. The U.S. Department of Labor reports that managers of retail stores, a similar management job, had a median income of $29,570 in 1998. The lowest paid 10 percent of this group earned approximately $16,700, while the highest paid 10 percent made approximately $71,910 annually. Generally, a salon manager's income will fall within this range. Salaries for salon managers will also depend on such factors as the location and size of the salon, the clientele, the services provided there, and the manager's experience. Depending on the salon, managers can earn a fixed salary or receive a percentage of the salon's profits. Fringe benefits, health and dental insurance, and paid vacation time are negotiated independently with each salon owner.

Work Environment

Much of managers' time is spent indoors establishing and maintaining relationships, and they should have a designated area or specific office space in which to confer with employees. They should be easily accessible to the public and still reach the far corners of the salon with ease. Since their presence is always known, they should look their best at all times, not always an easy task for busy directors who put in the longest hours.

The well-designed salon has a pleasing color scheme, an excellent floor plan, and possibly soothing music playing in the background and refreshments available for customers. It is part of the manager's responsibility to ensure a pleasant and sanitary atmosphere. While managers may receive some enjoyment from working in these surroundings, their jobs can also be quite hectic as they balance schedules, cover for sick employees, deal with demanding customers, or order supplies.

Outlook

The U.S. Department of Labor predicts job growth for barbers, cosmetologists, and other workers in the industry to be about as fast as the average through 2010. As long as the beauty industry continues its steady growth there will be opportunities for managers of salons. The Regis Corporation, the largest owner and franchiser of hair salons, currently operates and franchises over 3,600 salons and has approximately 29,000 employees worldwide. Despite these impressive numbers, however, President and CEO Paul Finkelstein sees room for expansion. As noted on the company Web site, Regis Corporation controls only 3 percent of the U.S. beauty market and plans to continue its growth. A major part of the beauty industry's success is due to the growing aging population and its desire to remain youthful.

For More Information

Contact this organization for industry news, a listing of accredited schools, and information on financial aid.

NATIONAL ACCREDITING COMMISSION OF COSMETOLOGY ARTS AND SCIENCES
901 North Stuart Street, Suite 900
Arlington, VA 22203
Tel: 703-527-7600
Web: http://www.naccas.org

This organization has news relating to government regulation of the industry.

PROFESSIONAL BEAUTY FEDERATION
2550 M Street, NW
Washington, DC 20037-1350
Web: http://www.probeautyfederation.org

This organization provides education and networking opportunities for its members.

THE SALON ASSOCIATION
15825 North 71st Street, Suite 100
Scottsdale, AZ 85254
Tel: 800-211-4872
Web: http://www.salons.org

This Web site provides a listing of schools by state.

BEAUTYSCHOOL.COM
Web: http://www.beautyschools.com

For hairstyling tips and techniques, job listings, and business advice, visit the following Web site:

BEHINDTHECHAIR
Web: http://www.behindthechair.com

Spa Attendants

Overview

Spa attendants work in hotels, resorts, and salons. They are specially trained in facial, body, and water treatments. They assist massage therapists and estheticians and prepare and clean the treatment rooms and tables. They provide spa customers with refreshments, towels, washcloths, and robes. According to *Lodging* magazine, there are approximately 5,700 spas in the United States.

History

Fossils prove that even the mammoths of over 20,000 years ago enjoyed a good spa treatment. The town of Hot Springs, a small resort village nestled in the hills of South Dakota, features a fossil excavation site; this site serves as evidence that mammoths were attracted to the area's pools of warm water. Humans share this attraction. Native Americans considered natural hot springs to be sacred healing grounds. All through Europe, the ancient Romans built colossal spas, including the Baths of Caracalla, one of the seven wonders of the world. Only its ruins remain, but Caracalla once featured hot and cold baths, a swimming pool, a gymnasium, shops, art galleries, and acres of gardens.

Although spas fell out of favor during the Middle Ages, by the 17th and 18th centuries they had once again become popular in Europe. An interest in making use of natural resources for healing and relaxation spread, and by the late 1800s there was hardly a well of natural spring water in the United States that a businessman hadn't capitalized upon. At the turn of the century in the United States, people visited resorts and spas (with or without natural hot springs) for exercise and relaxation. By the 1920s spas had become popular retreats for the wealthy. Since that time, spas have diversified their services and attracted a wide range of visitors. Today's spas have clients ranging from busy professionals looking for several hours of stress reduction, to families looking for healthy vacations, to pregnant women seeking relaxation, to men looking to keep fit. Over 95 million Americans visited a spa in 2001, according to a survey by PricewaterhouseCoopers (and reported in *Lodging* magazine).

The Job

From the ylang ylang plant to the lomilomi massage, spa attendants are teaching vacationers a new language of health and rejuvenation. Although there were only 30 spas in the United States in the late 1970s, the number now has grown past 5,000. Spas and resorts have cropped up around natural hot springs, the seaside, the desert, the mountains, and even the plains. Some spas are designed to meet very specific needs, such as weight management and holistic wellness. While most spas offer the usual facials, body wraps, and massages, many are expanding to include "mind/body awareness" as people flock to spas for both physical and spiritual needs. In some spas, you can schedule hypnosis, yoga, and dream therapy sessions right after your horseback riding, tennis game, and round of golf. So the duties of a spa attendant can vary greatly from location to location. Spa attendants are also finding work outside of the vacation industry, at salons and "day spas," as cosmetologists recognize the need to expand into other areas of beauty care. In addition to actually performing treatments, spa attendants devise special treatment plans for individual clients. They also schedule appointments, order and sell products, launder linens, and clean all spa areas. They offer advice on treatments and skin care products.

Craig Rabago works as a men's spa technician for the Ihilani Resort and Spa in Kapolei, Hawaii. *Ihilani* means "heavenly splendor," and it is part of Rabago's job to help guests realize this splendor. "I create an atmosphere that is heavenly for them," Rabago explains. "I'm of Hawaiian descent and a local. I give people a warm welcome and make them feel at home." Rabago has been trained in a variety of services, including seaweed wraps, salt scrubs, and thalasso hydrotherapy (a fresh seawater massage). The Ihilani features a fitness center and separate spas for men and women; each spa includes a sauna, steam room, needle shower, hot tub, and cold plunge. For the popular "cool ti leaf wrap," Rabago prepares a table in one of the spa's private rooms, spreading out the long, frond-like Hawaiian ti leaves and treating them with special oils. When the guest arrives for his wrap, Rabago gives him a robe and sandals and shows him to the lockers, then the showers. When the guest is ready for the treatment, Rabago then brings him to the treatment room and directs him to lie back on the table. As he explains the treatment, Rabago rubs the guest's skin with oils and lotions, making sure to pay special attention to sunburn, dry skin, and other trouble areas. He then wraps the guest in a damp sheet. Rabago leaves him wrapped for 25 minutes, checking in occasionally to make sure the guest is comfortable. In between treatments, Rabago must take linen inventory and keep the spa areas clean. He also does a fair amount of work on the computer. "But taking care of the guests' needs—that's my priority," Rabago says.

The Ihilani capitalizes on its locale, providing treatments with fresh sea water, sea salt, seaweed, and Hawaiian plants. In a different kind of environment, a spa and resort may provide very different services. Mud baths, natural hot spring whirlpools, volcanic mineral treatment—resort owners around the world develop their spas with the natural surroundings in mind. This results in very specific training for spa attendants. "The training was time-consuming," Rabago recalls. "The spa techs train with each other. We put in lots of hours of practice before we actually go to work on a guest."

Requirements

HIGH SCHOOL
To prepare for work as a spa attendant, take high school courses in anatomy, physiology, and biology. These classes will give you an understanding of the human body and muscle systems. Chemistry will prepare you for the use and preparation of skin care products. Health courses will teach you about nutrition, fitness, and other issues of importance to the health-conscious patrons of resorts and spas. Because so many spas offer treatment for both the body and the mind, take some psychology courses to learn about the history of treating depression, anxiety, and other mental and emotional problems. Finally, take computer classes, which will allow you to become comfortable using this technology. If in

your future job you need to keep track of spa supplies, you will probably be using a computer to do so.

In addition to these classes, you will benefit from having CPR and first aid training. Check with your high school to find out if it offers such training or contact organizations such as your local Red Cross. Many spas require attendants to know CPR and first aid, and your training will give you an advantage when looking for a job. Currently no specific postsecondary training program exists for spa attendants. Most spas put new hires through their own attendant training programs. Any work experience that you already have in a spa, therefore, will make you an appealing job candidate. During your high school years, try to get a summer job at one of the many resorts across the country. Spas often hire extra help to deal with the increased number of guests during this peak vacation period. Although you may be working only with the laundry, you will have the opportunity to see how a spa or resort is run and find out about the many different jobs available.

Some spas require their attendants to be certified cosmeticians or massage therapists. In such cases, education beyond high school is required. If you know of a specific spa at which you wish to work, ask about the hiring policy for attendants. Cosmeticians receive their training from cosmetology schools; massage therapists are educated at schools of massage therapy. Licensing requirements for these professionals vary by state, and you should know what these requirements are before you begin a program of study.

OTHER REQUIREMENTS

Craig Rabago of the Ihilani advises that a good spa attendant should "be happy, courageous, and ambitious." Guests of resorts and spas expect to be pampered and welcomed and can fully relax during a spa treatment only if the attendant is calm and considerate. Be prepared to serve your clients and to remain friendly and helpful. "But don't be timid and shy," Rabago says. "This is a good way to meet people from all around the world. You can broaden your horizons."

Any shyness and excessive modesty may also prevent you from performing your spa duties properly. You'll be applying lotions and oils to the naked skin of your guests—if you're uncomfortable, your clients will detect it and become uncomfortable themselves. You must take a professional approach so that your clients feel safe and at ease. You should have a good "bedside manner"—the calm, comforting approach health care professionals use. Self-confidence is also important; you must convey to your client that you're knowledgeable about the treatment.

Exploring

One of the best ways to explore this type of work is to get a part-time or summer job at a spa. You may be surprised by the number of spas in your area. There may even be a resort on the outskirts of your city. Look in the yellow pages under "Beauty Salons and Services" as well as "Health Clubs" and "Massage." (Many of the listings under "Spa" are only for hot tub dealerships.) Visit a salon or day spa and ask to interview someone who works as a spa attendant. Some attendants may allow you to shadow them for a day or two. Larger salons may have openings for part-time attendants, allowing you to gather firsthand experience.

Many resorts across the country advertise nationally for summer help. Check the classifieds of vacation and travel magazines, and visit http://www.resortjobs.com for a listing. You could also select a resort and spa from the pages of a tourism publication, such as *Resorts and Great Hotels* (http://www.resortsgreathotels.com), and call the hotel directly to request information about summer jobs. *Spa Finder* (http://www.spafinders.com) magazine also publishes a directory of spas.

If you are unable to find a job at a spa, consider a part-time or summer job at such places as a local hotel, beauty salon, or tanning salon. In any of these locations you will gain experience working with guests and providing for their comfort. Nursing homes and hospitals also employ high school students to provide clients or patients with personal care services. Working at a retail store specializing in products for skin care and beauty, aromatherapy, and massage can teach you about various spa treatments and products and help you decide if you are interested in this line of work.

If you have the money, consider making an appointment for yourself at a spa in your area. You may not be able to afford a vacation or full-day treatment, but even an hour spent as a client at a spa can give you an impression of what working in such an environment would be like.

Employers

The primary employers of spa attendants are hotels, resorts, salons, and, naturally, spas. Increasing numbers of salons are adding spas to their facilities to maintain a competitive edge; this will lead to increased opportunities for spa attendants throughout the country, mostly in larger cities and metropolitan areas. The same is true for hotel spas. Many spas, however, are clustered in resort areas with attractions such as hot springs and consistently pleasant climates.

Starting Out

Many spa attendants receive their training on the job, but some background experience in health care or cosmetology may help you in landing that first job as a spa attendant. Craig Rabago, for example, worked as a surgical aide before going to work for the Ihilani. "The work is related," he says, "but it's a very different atmosphere." He learned about the spa job from a listing in the newspaper. If you're not particular about your geographic location, check travel publications for listings of resorts and spas, or visit http://www.spafinders.com on the Web, and contact the spas about job openings. *Spa Finder,* both online and in its print directory, lists spas according to their specialties and locations.

A degree from a cosmetology or massage therapy school can be valuable when looking for a job in a spa. Many of these degree programs require field work, or hands-on experience, and they will put you in touch with salons and fitness centers. Without a degree, you may be limited in the spa treatments you're allowed to perform. But, as more and more individual hairstylists and beauty salons open day spas to accommodate all the needs of their clients, both licensed and unlicensed spa attendants will find more job opportunities.

Advancement

The longer an attendant works in a spa, the more he or she will learn about the services provided there. The attendant will also have more opportunities to expand upon the on-the-job training and potentially be allowed to perform more treatments. Though attendants typically start off with only an hourly wage, they can eventually receive commissions and tips. The more guests an attendant works with, the better tips and commission he or she will make. In a salon or day spa situation, the clientele will include regular customers. If they are happy with an attendant's work, they will request that attendant's services specifically and thus increase the attendant's income.

Attendants who complete further formal education also become qualified for more advanced positions. Those who attend cosmetology school to become cosmeticians typically have classes such as anatomy, chemistry, and physiology. They are qualified to work on the skin, giving facials, body wraps, and makeup applications, and they may also do hair removal by waxing or plucking. Nail technician programs offered through cosmetology schools or nail schools qualify the graduate to give manicures and pedicures. Attendants who are particularly interested in fitness may want to consider advancement by getting an associate's degree from a fitness program. Courses for such programs include muscle conditioning, nutrition, and injury prevention. Those interested in massage may seek advancement by completing a massage therapy school program, which will qualify them to give different types of massage. These programs include course work in anatomy and physiology as well as provide hands-on training.

Some attendants advance to become spa program directors. As program directors, they are responsible for adding new services, training spa attendants, determining what skin products to use, and controlling other details of the spa's daily practices. Those who wish to run their own businesses may eventually open their own spas.

Earnings

Salaries for spa attendants vary greatly across the country, so no significant salary survey has been conducted in recent years. Spa attendants make from minimum wage to around $10 per hour. Salaries vary according to work environment (a large resort will pay more than a small salon) and the spa attendant's responsibilities. Spa attendants are paid either by the hour or by commission (a percentage of the spa treatments performed). Spa attendants also receive tips of between 10 and 15 percent. Some spas automatically bill guests an additional percentage to cover the tip so that the guest doesn't have to worry about having the money on hand to give to the attendant. With tips from a wealthy clientele and a commission on higher-priced services, a spa attendant at a fine hotel will make much more than an attendant in a smaller day spa. Employees of spas are likely to receive better benefits than many of their counterparts in the cosmetology field. Spa attendants working at hotels may also receive a variety of perks, such as discounted spa treatments, guest rooms, meals in the hotel restaurants, and travel packages.

Work Environment

Working among vacationers in a sunny, scenic part of the world can be very enjoyable. Most spa attendants work within well-decorated, temperature-controlled buildings, with soothing music piped through the speaker systems. Fresh fruit, tea, and other refreshments are often readily available. Spa attendants work directly with a public that has come to a resort to alleviate stress and other worries, making for very relaxed interactions. Some hotel spa attendants even live on the premises in special employee quarters, or in nearby housing, allowing them to live close to the beaches, mountains, or whatever natural beauty surrounds the resort.

Because spas usually open in the wee hours of the morning and close after dark, spa attendants may have to work long, irregular hours. Depending on the codes of the spa, they wear uniforms and jackets. They also wear gloves if their skin is sensitive to some of the products.

In a local beauty salon, a spa attendant tries to maintain a similarly relaxed environment in the few rooms dedicated to spa treatment. The rest of the salon, however, may be noisy with waiting customers, hair dryers, electric clippers, and music. The salon may also affect those with allergies to chemicals in hair treatment products.

Day spas, which may be located in large cities, typically strive to maintain a serene environment for the clientele, from the reception area, where soft music may be playing in the background, to the private treatment rooms, which may have soft lighting. While the spa attendant may work in these areas, he or she is also part of the activity behind the scenes, often working with damp laundry, cleaning supplies, and spa products.

Outlook

The International SPA Association (ISPA) reports there were 1,783 spa facilities and providers in 55 nations as members in late November 2001, 27 percent more than the preceding year. Spas are offering more services to attract a variety of clients. The ISPA reports that men made up 28 percent of spa visitors in 2001, up from 23 percent in 1998. Many spas are adding treatments specifically for them. These expanding facilities and new treatment options should translate into job opportunities for everyone working in this industry, including spa attendants.

In addition, the public is becoming more health conscious, and people are looking to spas for both enjoyable and educational vacations. Some spas are specializing in teaching guests new patterns of diet, exercise, and skin care. A number of health care professionals are even predicting that spas will be covered by health insurance plans; doctors will write prescriptions to patients for spa treatments. To compete with other spas, and to satisfy returning guests, spas are likely to offer even more diverse lists of services and treatments. The spa attendant will have to keep ahead of health and beauty trends and be capable of adapting to new programs and methods.

Anticipating a future of one-stop beauty treatment, the owners of hair and beauty salons are dedicating rooms to spa treatments. For the cost of a little remodeling, hair salons can stay competitive with local day spas as well as generate more business. Spa attendants may find their best job opportunities at these salons, where they can earn a good commission and establish a client base.

For More Information

For employment opportunities, contact:
DAY SPA ASSOCIATION
310 17th Street
Union City, NJ 07087
Tel: 201-865-2065
Web: http://www.dayspaassociation.com

SPA SALON STAFFING SERVICES
PO Box 6831
Mesa, AZ 85216-6831
Tel: 888-736-1711
Web: http://www.spasalonstaffing.com

For more information on the spa industry, contact:
INTERNATIONAL SPA ASSOCIATION
2365 Harrodsburg Road, Suite A325
Lexington, KY 40504
Tel: 888-651-4772
Web: http://www.experienceispa.com

For information on accredited cosmetology schools and financial aid, contact:
NATIONAL ACCREDITING COMMISSION OF COSMETOLOGY ARTS AND SCIENCES
4401 Ford Avenue, Suite 1300
Alexandria, VA 22302-1432
Tel: 703-527-7600
Web: http://www.naccas.org

State Boards of Cosmetology

ALABAMA

ALABAMA STATE BOARD OF COSMETOLOGY
100 North Union Street, Suite 320
Montgomery, AL 36130
Tel: 334-242-1918
Email: cosmetology@aboc.state.al.us
Web: http://www.aboc.state.al.us
Occupational Fields: cosmetologist, esthetician, nail technician

ALASKA

ALASKA BOARD OF BARBERS AND HAIRDRESSERS
Division of Occupational Licensing
PO Box 110806
Juneau, AK 99811-0806
Tel: 907-465-2547
Email: cindy_evens@commerce.state.ak.us
Web: http://www.dced.state.ak.us/occ/pbah.htm
Occupational Fields: cosmetician, esthetician, hairdresser, manicurist

ARIZONA

ARIZONA STATE BOARD OF COSMETOLOGY
1721 East Broadway Road
Tempe, AZ 85282-1611
Tel: 480-784-4539
Occupational Fields: cosmetologist, esthetician, nail technician

ARKANSAS

ARKANSAS STATE BOARD OF COSMETOLOGY
101 East Capitol, #108
Little Rock, AR 72201
Tel: 501-682-2168
Web: http://www.accessarkansas.org/cos
Occupational Fields: cosmetologist, electrologist, esthetician, nail technician

CALIFORNIA

CALIFORNIA BARBERING AND COSMETOLOGY PROGRAM
PO Box 944226
Sacramento, CA 94244-2260
Tel: 800-952-5210
Web: http://www.dca.ca.gov/barber
Occupational Fields: barber, cosmetologist, electrologist, esthetician, manicurist

COLORADO

OFFICE OF BARBERS AND COSMETOLOGIST LICENSING
1560 Broadway, Suite 1340
Denver, CO 80202
Tel: 303-894-7772
Email: barber-cosmetology@dora.state.co.us
Web: http://www.dora.state.co.us/barbers_cosmetologists
Occupational Fields: barber, cosmetician, cosmetologist, manicurist

CONNECTICUT

CONNECTICUT DEPARTMENT OF PUBLIC HEALTH
Cosmetology & Licensing
410 Capitol Avenue, MS #12 APP
Hartford, CT 06134
Tel: 860-509-7569
Occupational Fields: cosmetologist, nail technician

DELAWARE

DELAWARE BOARD OF COSMETOLOGY AND BARBERING
Cannon Building, #203, PO Box 1401
Dover, DE 19903
Tel: 302-739-4522
Email: swolfe@state.de.us
Web: http://www.state.de.us/research/profreg/Frame.htm
Occupational Fields: cosmetologist, manicurist

DISTRICT OF COLUMBIA

DISTRICT OF COLUMBIA DEPARTMENT OF CONSUMER & REGULATORY AFFAIRS
Board of Barbering and Cosmetology
614 H Street, NW, #904
Washington, DC 20001
Tel: 202-727-7474
Web: http://dcra.dc.gov/information/build_pla/occupational/boards/barber.shtm
Occupational Fields: cosmetologist, manicurist, skin care specialist

FLORIDA

FLORIDA DEPARTMENT OF BUSINESS AND PROFESSIONAL REGULATION
Attn: Cosmetology
1940 North Monroe Street
Tallahassee, FL 32399
Tel: 850-487-1395
Web: http://www.state.fl.us/dbpr
Occupational Fields: cosmetologist, nail specialist, skin care specialist

GEORGIA

GEORGIA STATE BOARD OF BARBERS
Georgia State Board of Cosmetology
166 Prior Street, SW
Atlanta, GA 31217-3858
Tel: 478-207-1430
Web: http://www.sos.state.ga.us/plb/barber_cosmet
Occupational Fields: cosmetologist, esthetician, nail technician

HAWAII

HAWAII BOARD OF COSMETOLOGY
Department of Commerce and Consumer Affairs
PO Box 3469
Honolulu, HI 96801
Tel: 808-586-3000
Web: http://www.state.hi.us/dcca/pvl/areas_barbering.html
Occupational Fields: barber, cosmetologist, esthetician, nail technician

IDAHO

IDAHO STATE BOARD OF COSMETOLOGY
Bureau of Occupational Licenses
1109 Main Street, Suite 220
Boise, ID 83702-5642
Tel: 208-334-3233
Email: lfish@ibol.state.id.us
Web: http://www2.state.id.us/ibol/cos.htm
Occupational Fields: cosmetologist, esthetician, nail technician

IDAHO STATE BOARD OF BARBER EXAMINERS
Bureau of Occupational Licenses
1109 Main Street, Suite 220
Boise, ID 83702-5642
Tel: 208-334-3233
Email: mlondon@ibol.state.id.us
Occupational Fields: barber

ILLINOIS

ILLINOIS DEPARTMENT OF PROFESSIONAL REGULATION
320 West Washington Street
Springfield, IL 62786
Tel: 217-782-8556
Web: http://www.dpr.state.il.us
Occupational Fields: cosmetologist, esthetician, nail technician

INDIANA

INDIANA PROFESSIONAL LICENSING AGENCY
Indiana State Board of Barber Examiners
Indiana State Board of Cosmetology Examiners
302 West Washington, Room EO-34
Indianapolis, IN 46204-2700
Tel: 317-232-2980
Web: http://www.state.in.us/pla
Occupational Fields: cosmetologist, esthetician, manicurist

IOWA

IOWA DEPARTMENT OF PUBLIC HEALTH
Board of Cosmetology Arts and Sciences
321 East 12th Street, 4th Floor
Des Moines, IA 50319-0075
Tel: 515-281-3121
Email: scook@idph.state.ia.us
Occupational Fields: cosmetician, esthetician, nail technician

KANSAS

KANSAS STATE BOARD OF COSMETOLOGY
714 SW Jackson, Suite 100
Topeka, KS 66603-3230
Tel: 785-296-3155
Email: kboc@inc.org
Web: http://www.ink.org/public/kboc/
Occupational Fields: cosmetologist, electrologist, esthetician, nail technician

KENTUCKY

KENTUCKY BOARD OF BARBERING
9114 Leesgate, Suite 6
Louisville, KY 40222-5055
Tel: 502-429-5223
Occupational Fields: barber

KENTUCKY STATE BOARD OF HAIRDRESSERS &
COSMETOLOGISTS
III St. James Court
Frankfort, KY 40601
Tel: 502-564-4262
Occupational Fields: cosmetologist, nail technician

LOUISIANA

LOUISIANA STATE BOARD OF COSMETOLOGY
11622 Sunbelt Court
Baton Rouge, LA 70809
Tel: 225-756-3404
Occupational Fields: barber, cosmetologist, esthetician, nail technician

MAINE

MAINE STATE BOARD OF BARBERING & COSMETOLOGY
Department of Professional and Financial Regulation
Office of Licensing and Registration
35 State House Station
Augusta, ME 04333-0035
Tel: 207-624-8612
Email: soyna.m.weed@state.me.us
Web: http://www.state.me.us/pfr/olr/list.htm
Occupational Fields: barber, cosmetologist, esthetician, nail technician

MARYLAND

MARYLAND STATE BOARD OF BARBERS
Maryland State Board of Cosmetologists
500 North Calvert Street, Room 307
Baltimore, MD 21202-3651
Tel: 410-230-6320
Web: http://www.dllr.state.md.us/license/occprof/cos.html
Occupational Fields: cosmetologist, electrologist, esthetician,
nail technician

MASSACHUSETTS

MASSACHUSETTS DIVISION OF PROFESSIONAL LICENSURE
Board of Cosmetology
239 Causeway Street, Suite 500
Boston, MA 02114
Tel: 617-727-9940
Email: kim.m.scully@state.ma.us
Web: http://www.state.ma.us/reg/boards/hd
Occupational Fields: cosmetologist, electrologist, esthetician,
nail technician

MICHIGAN

MICHIGAN STATE BOARD OF COSMETOLOGY
Bureau of Commercial Services, Licensing Division
PO Box 30018
Lansing, MI 48909
Tel: 517-241-9201
Email: bcsinfo@cis.state.mi.us
Web: http://www.cis.state.mi.us/bcs/cos/site.htm
Occupational Fields: barber, cosmetologist, electrologist, esthetician,
manicurist

MINNESOTA

MINNESOTA DEPARTMENT OF COMMERCE
Licensing Division, Cosmetology Unit
133 East 7th Street
St. Paul, MN 55101
Tel: 651-296-6319
Email: licensing@state.mn.us
Web: http://www.dted.state.mn.us
Occupational Fields: cosmetologist, esthetician, manicurist

BOARD OF BARBER EXAMINERS
1885 University Avenue
St. Paul, MN 55104
Tel: 651-642-0489
Web: http://www.dted.state.mn.us
Occupational Fields: barber, barber apprentice, barber instructor

MISSISSIPPI

MISSISSIPPI STATE BOARD OF COSMETOLOGY
PO Box 55689
Jackson, MS 39296-5689
Tel: 601-987-6837
Occupational Fields: cosmetologist, esthetician, nail technician

MISSOURI

MISSOURI BOARD OF BARBER EXAMINERS
3605 Missouri Boulevard
PO Box 1335
Jefferson City, MO 65102-1335
Tel: 800-735-2966
Email: barber@mail.state.mo.us
Web: http://www.ecodev.state.mo.us/pr
Occupational Fields: barber

MISSOURI STATE BOARD OF COSMETOLOGY
PO Box 1062
Jefferson City, MO 65102
Tel: 573-751-1052
Email: cosmo@mail.state.mo.us
Web: http://www.ded.state.mo.us/regulatorylicensing/
professionalregistration/cosmo
Occupational Fields: cosmetologist, manicurist

MISSOURI STATE BOARD OF THERAPEUTIC MASSAGE
PO Box 1335
Jefferson City, MO 65102-1335
Tel: 573-522-6277
Email: massagetherapy@mail.state.mo.us
Web: http://www.ecodev.state.mo.us/pr
Occupational Fields: massage therapist

MONTANA

MONTANA BOARD OF BARBERS
Montana Department of Commerce
Division of Professional & Occupational Licensing
301 South Park
PO Box 200513
Helena, MT 59620-0513
Tel: 406-841-2333
Email: compolbar@state.mt.us
Web: http://www.com.state.mt.us/License/POL/licensing_boards.htm
Occupational Fields: barber

MONTANA DEPARTMENT OF COMMERCE
Board of Cosmetologists
301 South Park, 4th Floor
PO Box 200513
Helena, MT 59620-0513
Tel: 406-841-2730
Email: compolcos@state.mt.us
Web: http://www.com.state.mt.us/License/POL/licensing_boards.htm
Occupational Fields: cosmetologist, electrologist, esthetician, manicurist, nail technician

NEBRASKA

NEBRASKA DEPARTMENT OF HEALTH & HUMAN SERVICES
Regulation & Licensure Credentialing Division
PO Box 95007
Lincoln, NE 68509-5007
Tel: 402-471-2117
Email: doh6121@vmhost.cdp.state.ne.us
Occupational Fields: cosmetologist, electrologist, esthetician

NEVADA

NEVADA STATE BOARD OF COSMETOLOGY
1785 East Sahara Avenue, #255
Las Vegas, NV 89104
Tel: 702-486-6542
Occupational Fields: cosmetologist, electrologist, esthetician, hair designer, manicurist

NEW HAMPSHIRE

BOARD OF BARBERING, COSMETOLOGY, AND ESTHETICS
2 Industrial Park Drive
Concord, NH 03301
Tel: 603-271-3608
Web: http://www.state.nh.us/cosmet
Occupational Fields: barber, cosmetologist, esthetician, manicurist

NEW JERSEY

NEW JERSEY STATE BOARD OF COSMETOLOGY AND HAIRSTYLING
PO Box 45003
Newark, NJ 07101
Tel: 973-504-6400
Email: askconsumeraffairs@dca.lps.state.nj.us
Web: http://www.state.nj.us/lps/ca
Occupational Fields: barber, cosmetologist, cosmetologist instructor, manicurist, skin care specialist

NEW MEXICO

NEW MEXICO BARBER AND COSMETOLOGIST BOARD
2055 Pacheco Street, Suite 400
Santa Fe, NM 87504
Web: http://www.rld.state.nm.us/b&c/barber_and_cosmetologist_board.htm
Occupational Fields: barber, cosmetologist, electrologist, esthetician, manicurist-pedicurist

NEW YORK

NEW YORK DEPARTMENT OF STATE
Division of Licensing Services
84 Holland Avenue
Albany, NY 12208-3490
Tel: 518-474-4429
Email: licensing@dos.state.ny.us
Web: http://www.dos.state.ny.us/lcns/licensing.html
Occupational Fields: barber, cosmetologist, esthetician, nail technician

NORTH CAROLINA

**NORTH CAROLINA STATE BOARD OF COSMETIC ART
EXAMINERS**
1201 Front Street, #110
Raleigh, NC 27609-7533
Tel: 919-733-4117
Web: http://www.cosmetology.state.nc.us
Occupational Fields: cosmetologist, esthetician, manicurist

NORTH DAKOTA

NORTH DAKOTA STATE BOARD OF COSMETOLOGY
1102 South Washington Street
Bismarck, ND 58504
Tel: 701-224-9800
Occupational Fields: cosmetologist, manicurist

OHIO

OHIO STATE BOARD OF COSMETOLOGY
101 Southland Mall
Columbus, OH 43207-4041
Tel: 614-466-3834
Email: ohiocosbd@das.state.oh.us
Web: http://www.state.oh.us/cos/licensedb.htm
Occupational Fields: cosmetologist, manicurist

OKLAHOMA

OKLAHOMA STATE BOARD OF COSMETOLOGY
2200 Classen Boulevard, #1530
Oklahoma City, OK 73106
Tel: 405-521-2441
Email: bmoore@oklaosf.state.ok.us
Web: http://www.state.ok.us/~cosmo
Occupational Fields: cosmetologist, manicurist

OREGON

OREGON BOARD OF BARBERS & HAIRDRESSERS
Health Division
700 Summer Street, NE, Suite 320
Salem, OR 97301-1287
Tel: 503-378-8667
Email: hdlp.mail@state.or.us
Web: http://www.hdlp.hr.state.or.us
Occupational Fields: barber, cosmetologist, electrologist, nail technician, permanent color technician

PENNSYLVANIA

STATE BOARD OF BARBER EXAMINERS
PO Box 2649
Harrisburg, PA 17105-2649
Tel: 717-783-3402
Email: barber@pados.dos.state.pa.us
Web: http://www.dos.state.pa.us/bpoa
Occupational Fields: barber

STATE BOARD OF COSMETOLOGY
Bureau of Professional and Occupational Affairs
PO Box 2649
Harrisburg, PA 17105-2649
Tel: 717-783-7130
Email: bpoa@pados.state.pa.us
Web: http://www.dos.state.pa.us/bpoa
Occupational Fields: cosmetologist, manicurist

RHODE ISLAND

DEPARTMENT OF HEALTH, DIVISION OF HAIRDRESSING AND BARBERING
Rhode Island State Division of Professional Licensing
3 Capitol Hill, Room 104
Providence, RI 02908-5097
Tel: 401-222-2511
Web: http://www.healthri.org/hsr/regulations/hair_barber.pdf
Occupational Fields: barber, cosmetologist, esthetician, hairdresser instructor, manicurist

SOUTH CAROLINA

DEPARTMENT OF LABOR, LICENSING, AND REGULATION
Board of Barber Examiners
PO Box 11329
Columbia, SC 29211
Tel: 803-896-4491
Web: http://www.llr.state.sc.us/POL/Cosmetology
Occupational Fields: barber

BOARD OF COSMETOLOGY
PO Box 11329
Columbia, SC 29211
Tel: 803-896-4568
Email: jonese@mail.llr.state.sc.us
Web: http://www.llr.state.sc.us/POL/Cosmetology
Occupational Fields: cosmetologist, esthetician, nail technician

DEPARTMENT OF LABOR, LICENSING, AND REGULATION
Massage/Bodywork Therapy
PO Box 11329
Columbia, SC 29211
Tel: 803-896-4588
Email: jonese@mail.llr.state.sc.us
Web: http://www.llr.state.sc.us/mbt.htm
Occupational Fields: massage therapist

SOUTH DAKOTA

SOUTH DAKOTA BOARD OF BARBER EXAMINERS
PO Box 1115
Pierre, SD 57501-1115
Tel: 605-224-6281
Email: jdamonlaw@aol.com
Web: http://www.state.sd.us/dcr/barber
Occupational Fields: barber

SOUTH DAKOTA COSMETOLOGY COMMISSION
500 East Capitol Avenue
Pierre, SD 57501-5070
Tel: 605-773-6193
Email: cosmetology@state.sd.us
Web: http://www.state.sd.us/dcr/cosmo
Occupational Fields: cosmetologist, nail technician

TENNESSEE

TENNESSEE STATE BOARD OF COSMETOLOGY
500 James Robertson Parkway
Nashville, TN 37243-1147
Tel: 800-480-9285
Email: egriffin@mail.state.tn.us
Web: http://www.state.tn.us/commerce/cosmo
Occupational Fields: cosmetologist, esthetician, nail technician

TEXAS

TEXAS STATE BOARD OF BARBER EXAMINERS
5717 Balcones Drive
Austin, TX 78731-4203
Tel: 512-458-0111
Email: will.brown@tsbbe.state.tx.us
Web: http://www.tsbbe.state.tx.us
Occupational Fields: barber

TEXAS COSMETOLOGY COMMISSION
5717 Balcones Drive
Austin, TX 78731-4203
Tel: 800-943-8922
Email: Elizabeth.perez@txcc.state.tx.us
Web: http://www.txcc.state.tx.us
Occupational Fields: cosmetologist, esthetician, nail technician

UTAH

UTAH STATE BOARD OF COSMETOLOGY

Division of Occupational and Professional Licensing
160 East 300 South
PO Box 45805
Salt Lake City, UT 84145-0805
Tel: 801-530-6628
Email: cormond@br.state.ut.us
Web: http://www.dopl.utah.gov/licensing/cosmetology.html
Occupational Fields: barber, cosmetologist, barber/cosmetologist instructor, electrologist, electrologist instructor, esthetician, nail technologist, nail technologist instructor, massage therapist

VERMONT

BOARD OF BARBERS AND COSMETOLOGISTS

Office of Professional Regulation
26 Terrace Street, Drawer 09
Montpelier, VT 05609-1101
Tel: 802-828-2837
Email: nmorin@secstate.vt.us
Web: http://vtprofessionals.org
Occupational Fields: barber, cosmetologist, electrologist, esthetician, manicurist

VIRGINIA

VIRGINIA BOARD OF COSMETOLOGY

Department of Professional and Occupational
3600 West Broad Street
Richmond, VA 23230-4917
Tel: 804-367-8509
Email: barbercosmo@dpor.state.va.us
Web: http://www.state.va.us/dpor/cos_main.htm
Occupational Fields: barber, cosmetologist, manicurist

WASHINGTON

WASHINGTON STATE DEPARTMENT OF LICENSING
Division of Professional Licensing
PO Box 9026
Olympia, WA 98507-9026
Tel: 360-664-6626
Email: plss@dol.wa.gov
Web: http://www.dol.wa.gov/plss/cosfront.htm
Occupational Fields: barber, cosmetologist, esthetician, manicurist

WEST VIRGINIA

WEST VIRGINIA BOARD OF BARBERS AND COSMETOLOGISTS
1716 Pennsylvania Avenue, #7
Charleston, WV 25302
Tel: 304-558-3450
Web: http://www.wvdhhr.org
Occupational Fields: cosmetologist, esthetician, nail technician

WISCONSIN

WISCONSIN BARBERING AND COSMETOLOGY EXAMINING BOARD
Wisconsin Department of Regulations and Licensing
PO Box 8935
Madison, WI 53708-8935
Tel: 608-266-5511
Web: http://www.drl.state.wi.us/Regulation
Occupational Fields: barber, cosmetologist, electrologist, esthetician, manicurist

WYOMING

WYOMING STATE BOARD OF COSMETOLOGY
2515 Warren Avenue, Suite 302
Cheyenne, WY 82002
Tel: 307-777-3534
Email: Babern@missc.state.wy.us
Web: http://soswy.state.wy.us/director/ag-bd/cosmet.htm
Occupational Fields: barber, cosmetologist, manicurist, nail technician

Index

aestheticians, 47
aromatherapists, 5-16

barbers, 17-24, 62
barber-stylists, 17
beauticians, 63
beauty advisers, 57
bodyworkers, 103

color analysts, 25-32
cosmetic surgeons, 33-45
cosmeticians, 46-55
cosmetics sales representatives, 56-61
cosmetologists, 62-73

dermatoimmunologists, 76
dermatologic surgeons, 76
dermatologists, 74-83
dermatopathologists, 76
desairologists, 114

electrologists, 84-92
esthetic surgeons, 33
estheticians, 47

image consultants, 25-32

makeup artists, 93-102
manicurists, 125
massage therapists, 103-113
masseurs, 103
masseuses, 103
massotherapists, 103
mortuary cosmetologists, 114-124

nail artists, 125
nail sculpturists, 125
nail technicians, 125-135

occupational dermatologists, 77

pediatric dermatologists, 77
pedicurists, 125
plastic surgeons, 33

salon managers, 49, 136-144
salon owners, 49
skin care specialists, 47
spa attendants, 145-154

tonsorial artists, 17